Investing in Early Childhood Development

A WORLD BANK STUDY

Investing in Early Childhood Development

Review of the World Bank's Recent Experience

Rebecca K. Sayre, Amanda E. Devercelli,
Michelle J. Neuman, and Quentin Wodon

© 2015 International Bank for Reconstruction and Development / The World Bank
1818 H Street NW, Washington DC 20433
Telephone: 202-473-1000; Internet: www.worldbank.org

Some rights reserved

1 2 3 4 17 16 15 14

World Bank Studies are published to communicate the results of the Bank's work to the development community with the least possible delay. The manuscript of this paper therefore has not been prepared in accordance with the procedures appropriate to formally edited texts.

This work is a product of the staff of The World Bank with external contributions. The findings, interpretations, and conclusions expressed in this work do not necessarily reflect the views of The World Bank, its Board of Executive Directors, or the governments they represent. The World Bank does not guarantee the accuracy of the data included in this work. The boundaries, colors, denominations, and other information shown on any map in this work do not imply any judgment on the part of The World Bank concerning the legal status of any territory or the endorsement or acceptance of such boundaries.

Nothing herein shall constitute or be considered to be a limitation upon or waiver of the privileges and immunities of The World Bank, all of which are specifically reserved.

Rights and Permissions

This work is available under the Creative Commons Attribution 3.0 IGO license (CC BY 3.0 IGO) http://creativecommons.org/licenses/by/3.0/igo. Under the Creative Commons Attribution license, you are free to copy, distribute, transmit, and adapt this work, including for commercial purposes, under the following conditions:

Attribution—Please cite the work as follows: Sayre, Rebecca K., Amanda E. Devercelli, Michelle J. Neuman, and Quentin Wodon. 2015. *Investing in Early Childhood Development: Review of the World Bank's Recent Experience*. World Bank Studies. Washington, DC: World Bank. doi:10.1596/978-1-4648-0403-8. License: Creative Commons Attribution CC BY 3.0 IGO

Translations—If you create a translation of this work, please add the following disclaimer along with the attribution: *This translation was not created by The World Bank and should not be considered an official World Bank translation. The World Bank shall not be liable for any content or error in this translation.*

Adaptations—If you create an adaptation of this work, please add the following disclaimer along with the attribution: *This is an adaptation of an original work by The World Bank. Responsibility for the views and opinions expressed in the adaptation rests solely with the author or authors of the adaptation and are not endorsed by The World Bank.*

Third-party content—The World Bank does not necessarily own each component of the content contained within the work. The World Bank therefore does not warrant that the use of any third-party-owned individual component or part contained in the work will not infringe on the rights of those third parties. The risk of claims resulting from such infringement rests solely with you. If you wish to re-use a component of the work, it is your responsibility to determine whether permission is needed for that re-use and to obtain permission from the copyright owner. Examples of components can include, but are not limited to, tables, figures, or images.

All queries on rights and licenses should be addressed to the Publishing and Knowledge Division, The World Bank, 1818 H Street NW, Washington, DC 20433, USA; fax: 202-522-2625; e-mail: pubrights@worldbank.org.

ISBN (paper): 978-1-4648-0403-8
ISBN (electronic): 978-1-4648-0404-5
DOI: 10.1596/978-1-4648-0403-8

Cover photo: Children singing in a class at a public preschool in Vietnam. © Tran Thi Hoa / The World Bank. Used with permission. Further permission required for reuse.

Library of Congress Cataloging-in-Publication Data has been requested.

Contents

Acknowledgments		*ix*
Executive Summary		*xi*
	World Bank Support for ECD	xi
	World Bank Operational and Analytical Investments	xii
	Lessons Learned from ECD Operations	xiii
	Looking Forward	xiv
	Note	xiv
Abbreviations		*xv*
Chapter 1	Introduction	1
	Importance of Investing in ECD	1
	Note	4
Chapter 2	Methodology for the Study	5
	Abstract	5
	What Is Meant by ECD and Essential ECD Interventions?	5
	What Has Been Included in This Review and What Has Not?	7
	Note	10
Chapter 3	Trends in Operations	11
	Abstract	11
	IBRD/IDA Operations: Commitment Levels and Trends	11
	IBRD/IDA Commitments by Sector, Region, and Country Income	15
	ECD Share in Human Development IBRD/IDA Operations	18
	Trust-Funded ECD Operations	20
	Operations Likely to Benefit Children	21
Chapter 4	Case Studies of Operations	23
	Abstract	23
	Selection of the Case Studies	23
	Bulgaria Social Inclusion Project (SIP)	26

	Eritrea Integrated Early Child Development (IECD) Project	27
	Indonesia Early Childhood Education and Development (ECED) Project	29
	Jamaica Early Child Development (ECD) Project	30
	Jordan ECD Component of Education Reform for the Knowledge Economy	32
	Mexico ECD Component of Compensatory Education Project	33
	Senegal Nutrition Enhancement Program (Phases I and II)	35
	Note	36
Chapter 5	**Lessons Learned from Operations**	**37**
	Abstract	37
	Considerations for Effective ECD Project Design	37
	National Commitment	39
	Local Ownership	40
	Coordination across Sectors and Levels	41
	Targeting Disadvantaged Children	42
	Sociocultural Relevance	42
	Knowledge Exchange	43
	Note	44
Chapter 6	**Trends in Analytical, Advisory, and Partnership Work**	**45**
	Abstract	45
	Investments in Analytical, Advisory, and Partnership Work	45
	Analytical, Advisory, and Partnership Activities by Sector and Region	48
	ECD Share in HD Analytical and Partnership Activities	49
	Examples of Analytical, Advisory, and Partnership Work	51
	Note	54
Chapter 7	**Recent Initiatives**	**55**
	Abstract	55
	What Are the Challenges to Increasing Investment in ECD?	55
	New Initiatives and Opportunities to Expand ECD Investments	56
	Conclusion	62
Appendix A	Supporting Figures and Tables	63
Appendix B	Human Development ECD Project Portfolio	67
Appendix C	Snapshot of Case Studies of Operations	125
Bibliography		*135*

Box
2.1	Clarifying the Definition of ECD and Related Terms	6

Figures
2.1	Selection of Projects for This Review	9
3.1	IBRD/IDA ECD Operations in the HD Portfolio, US$ million (US$ of 2013)	13
3.2	IBRD/IDA ECD Operations in the HD Portfolio, Number	14
3.3	IBRD/IDA ECD Operations in ED, HNP, and SP US$ million (US$ of 2013)	14
3.4	IBRD/IDA Investment in ECD in the HD Portfolio Per Child under Five	17
3.5	Share of ECD Commitments in Overall HD Portfolio	19
3.6	Trust-funded ECD Operations in the HD Portfolio, US$ million (US$ of 2013)	21
6.1	HD ECD Analytical, Advisory, and Partnership Activities, US$ million (US$ of 2013)	47
6.2	Trend in Number of HD ECD Analytical, Advisory, and Partnership Activities	47
6.3	Share of Projects with ECD Components in HD Analytical/Partnership Portfolio	50
6.4	Share of Funding for Activities with ECD Components in HD Analytical/Partnership Portfolio	51
7.1	SABER-ECD Policy Goals and Levers	57
7.2	Five Packages of Essential ECD Services and Interventions	60

Maps
3.1	Global Distribution of HD ECD Investments through IBRD/IDA	16
6.1	Distribution of HD ECD Analytical, Advisory, and Partnership Activities	49
A.1	Distribution of HD IBRD/IDA ECD Commitments Per Child under Five	65

Tables
ES.1	Human Development Early Childhood Development Portfolio between FY 2001 and FY 2013	xii
3.1	Trend in the Number of IBRD/IDA Operations and Funding for ECD	12
3.2	IBRD/IDA Commitments (in US$ of 2013) to ECD by Region and Sector	16
3.3	Share of ECD in HD IBRD/IDA Portfolio by Time Period	19
3.4	Trust-funded Operations (in US$ of 2013) to ECD by Region and Sector	20
4.1	Summary of ECD Case Studies	24

5.1	Examples of PDO Indicators	39
6.1	Analytical, Advisory, and Partnership Activities, by Type (FY 2001 to FY 2013)	46
6.2	Trend in the Number of and Funding for ECD-Related Analytical and Partnership Activities by Year	46
6.3	Analytical, Advisory, and Partnership Activities: Number of Tasks and Funding (in US$ of 2013) by Region and Sector	48
6.4	Share of ECD in HD Analytical and Partnership Portfolio by Year	50
6.5	Ongoing SIEF-Funded ECD Impact Evaluations at the World Bank: First Round (2012): Early Childhood Nutrition, Health, and Development Cluster	52
6.6	Ongoing SIEF-Funded ECD Impact Evaluations at the World Bank: First Round (2012): Basic Education Service Delivery Cluster	53
7.1	eLearning Course on ECD for Policy makers and Practitioners	59
A.1	Investment in ECD Per Country, Per Person, and Per Poor Person, FY 2001 to FY 2011	63
A.2	New Ongoing SIEF-Funded Impact Evaluations at the World Bank: Second Round, 2013	65
B.1	Operations (Lending and Trust Funded)	68
B.2	Analytical Activities (Economic and Sector Work, Technical Assistance, Impact Evaluations, Knowledge Products, Global Partnership Programs, and Programmatic Approaches)	94
B.3	Projects Likely to Benefit Young Children (Lending and Trust Funded)	102
C.1	Snapshot of Case Studies of Operations	125

Acknowledgments

This report was prepared by a team comprising Rebecca K. Sayre, Amanda E. Devercelli, Michelle J. Neuman (task team leader until April 2013), and Quentin Wodon (task team leader after April 2013) under the guidance of Harry Patrinos and Elizabeth King. It is a collaborative product from three World Bank Global Practices for Education; Health, Nutrition, & Population; and Social Protection & Labor. Generous support from the Children's Investment Fund Foundation for the preparation of the report is gratefully acknowledged.

The report benefitted from comments from a number of colleagues including Leslie Elder, Peter Anthony Holland, Sachiko Kataoka, and Laura Rawlings, who served as peer reviewers, as well as Luis Benveniste, Plamen Danchev, Angela Demas, Amina Denboba, Carla Maria Paredes Drouet, Safaa El Tayeb El-Kogali, Marito Garcia, Amer Hasan, Tomomi Miyajima, Menno Mulder-Sibanda, Harriet Nannyonjo, Rosfita Roesli, Deepa Sankar, Prateek Tandon, and Julieta Trias. Any errors or omissions are those of the authors only.

Executive Summary

World Bank Support for ECD

The World Bank is actively supporting early childhood development based on demand from governments and convincing evidence on the benefits of investing early for children, families, and society.

This portfolio review provides an overview of Bank investments in early childhood development (ECD) from 2001 to 2013 within the three global practices of education (ED), health, nutrition, and population (HNP), and social protection and labor (SP).[1] In this report, we will consider the three global practices together as the "Human Development" (HD) portfolio of the World Bank. The report summarizes trends in operational and analytical investments in early childhood, including lending and trust-funded operations at the country, regional, and global levels. We present findings on the overall level of finance during this 13-year period, the number of ECD investments, and regional and sectoral trends. A series of case studies are presented to highlight lessons learned to inform future Bank support to ECD and to promote better planning across sectors and regions. We then present trends in analytical and advisory activities, including economic sector work, technical assistance, partnership activities, impact evaluations, programmatic approaches, and knowledge products. Finally, the paper discusses recent new approaches to support ECD within the World Bank and in client countries.

The World Bank works with countries through multiple entry points to invest in young children.

The HD ECD portfolio includes investments across the health, nutrition, and population, social protection and labor, and education practices, which can be grouped into the following general areas of focus:

- **Child nutrition**—including food fortification, community nutrition education, and food security
- **Maternal and child health**—including promotion of breastfeeding, prenatal care, newborn health, immunizations, and child survival
- **Early childhood care and education (ECCE)**—including preprimary education, school readiness, and parenting education
- **Family support and inclusion**—including social assistance, safety net, and conditional cash transfers (CCTs) to incentivize parents to invest in health

and education of their young children, primarily delivered through social protection sector
- Integrated/Multisectoral ECD projects and evaluations—including integrated health, nutrition, and education interventions, impact evaluations of ECD, and support to governments to improve ECD policies.

World Bank Operational and Analytical Investments

In the last 13 years, the World Bank invested $3.3 billion in 273 investments in ECD through the three HD practices.

HD ECD investments include 166 operations, including IBRD/IDA (International Bank for Reconstruction and Development/International Development Association) and trust-funded projects, which include both special financing and recipient executed opportunities. Additionally, during this time period, the three HD global practices invested in 107 analytical and advisory activities, including economic and sector work (ESW), Global Programs and Partnerships (GPP), technical assistance (TA), impact evaluations (IE), programmatic approaches (PA), and knowledge products (KP). Table ES.1 displays the breakdown of the three global practices' 273 investments, which supported 80 countries around the world.

In real terms, World Bank funding for ECD operations and analytical work increased from fiscal year (FY) 2001 to FY 2013; between FY 2001 and FY 2011 funding levels were fairly flat, with a big increase in FY 2012 and FY 2013.

Between 2001 and 2011, the number of operations remained at about 12 per year on average. During this time period, operational investments averaged $211 million per year (in 2013 US$). However, in 2012 and 2013, investments dramatically increased. In 2012, the three HD practices invested $524 million in 16 operations, and in 2013, they invested $707 million in 18 operations. In other

Table ES.1 Human Development Early Childhood Development Portfolio between FY 2001 and FY 2013

	Number of projects	Financing (in nominal US$ mil)	Financing (in 2013 US$ mil)
Operations (components and self-standing)			
IBRD/IDA	116	3,087.5	3,352.2
Trust funded	50	205.5	216.9
Analytical, advisory, and partnership activities			
Economic and sector work	32	6.6	7.1
Global programs and partnerships	8	11.9	13.7
Technical assistance	44	18.0	19.5
Impact evaluation	16	13.1	13.2
Programmatic approach	3	1.0	1.0
Knowledge product	4	0.8	0.9
TOTAL	273	3,344.5	3,624.5

Source: World Bank data.
Note: IBRD = International Bank for Reconstruction and Development; IDA = International Development Association.

words, both the number of operations and their size increased substantially in 2012 and 2013, as compared to the previous 10 years. The budget for analytical advisory activities (AAA) work has also increased, especially in 2013. Between 2001 and 2012, funding for analytical and advisory activities each year averaged $3.3 million through an average of six activities per year. In 2013, there were 31 analytical activities, with a total budget of $15 million. The increase in investments in ECD coincides with the adoption of a number of strategic World Bank documents in education, health-nutrition-population, and social protection-labor that have emphasized the importance of ECD.

All six World Bank regions are investing in ECD through both operational and analytical work; Africa and Latin America and the Caribbean are leading the way with the largest investments.

While all regions are investing, the Latin America and the Caribbean portfolio includes the largest operational investments ($1.3 billion invested through 42 projects). The Africa portfolio includes the most analytical activities ($19.8 million invested through 29 AAA tasks).

More than half of HD spending on ECD is through the HNP sector.

In terms of IBRD/IDA operations, a total of $2.2 billion in finance was allocated via HNP through 59 operations between FY 2001 and FY 2013. This is substantially more than ED, which invested $935 million through 42 operations and SP, which invested $241 million in ECD through 15 projects during the same period.

Lessons Learned from ECD Operations

This ECD portfolio review highlights six lessons to inform future work.

Upon reviewing the Bank's portfolio of ECD projects, we wish to highlight the following six specific lessons for Bank staff and partners to consider for future investments in ECD:

- Design of ECD projects, due to their complexity and the time lag between investments and impacts on children's development, requires careful attention to results frameworks, monitoring and evaluation, and a clear definition of roles and responsibilities of all actors within the project.
- Commitment from all levels of government as well as local communities is crucial.
- Parents are key stakeholders who should be included in ECD project design and implementation, as they can maintain and improve upon the gains from traditional ECD services delivered through a project.
- Coordination across sectors and levels is essential. The strategy for intersectoral coordination and identification of an institutional anchor depends on an individual country context. Existing ministerial and stakeholder relationships specific to the country context play a considerable role in affecting a project's success.

- Projects should be designed to ensure that quality interventions are accessible and culturally relevant to all children, particularly those who face the most obstacles.
- Knowledge exchange (for example, South-South activities) of positive project experience can be a valuable strategy to motivate governments to improve ECD systems as well as strengthen existing and future World Bank-supported ECD projects.

Looking Forward

The evidence on the returns to investments in ECD is clear. The demand for investments in ECD is rising within our client countries and, as a result, within the World Bank portfolio. Investing in ECD has high potential to help achieve the Bank's twin goals of eliminating poverty and increasing shared prosperity. Recently, the Bank has developed a series of new tools and mechanisms to support ECD through analytical work, project preparation, new partnerships, and innovative approaches.

Note

1. These three practices used to form the Human Development Network (HDN) at the World Bank.

Abbreviations

AAA	analytical advisory activities
ACGF	Africa Catalytic Growth Fund
BF	*Bolsa Familia*
CCT	conditional cash transfer
CEP	Compensatory Education Project (Mexico)
CFR	case fatality rate
CLM	Cellule de Lutte contre la Malnutrition (Coordination unit for the reduction of malnutrition) (Senegal)
CONAFE	Consejo Nacional Fomento Educación (National Council for Education Development) (Mexico)
CPP	Global Programs and Partnerships
DLI	disbursement-linked indicator
DRC	Democratic Republic of Congo
DUTCHP	Netherlands Partnership Program
EAP	East Asia and the Pacific
ECA	Europe and Central Asia
ECC	Early Childhood Commission (Jamaica)
ECCD	early childhood care and development
ECCE	early childhood care and education
ECD	early childhood development
ECDVU	Early Childhood Development Virtual University
ECE	early childhood education
ECED	early childhood education and development (project in Indonesia)
ED	education sector
EDI	Early Development Instrument
ELP	Early Learning Partnership
ERfKE	Education Reform for Knowledge Economy (Jordan)
ESW	economic and sector work
FPCR	Food Price Crisis Response

FTI	fast track initiative
FY	fiscal year
GDP	gross domestic product
GFCR	Global Food Crisis Response Program
GMP	Growth Monitoring Promotion
GoB	Government of Bulgaria
GoE	Government of Eritrea
GoI	Government of Indonesia
GoJ	Government of Jamaica
GoM	Government of Malawi
GoS	Government of Senegal
GPBA	Global Partnership on Output-based Aid
GPE	Global Partnership for Education
GPP	Global Partnership Program
HD	human development
HDN	Human Development Network
HDNED	HDN – Education Unit
HNP	health, nutrition, and population sector
IBRD	International Bank for Reconstruction and Development
ICMI	Integrated Management of Childhood Illnesses
ICR	Implementation Completion Results
IDA	International Development Association
IE	impact evaluation
IECD	Integrated Early Childhood Development (project in Eritrea)
ISR	Implementation Status and Results
ITN	insecticide-treated bed net
JSDF	Japan Social Development Fund
KG	kindergarten
KP	knowledge product
LAC	Latin America and the Caribbean
M&E	monitoring and evaluation
MNA	Middle East and North Africa
MoE	Ministry of Education
NEP	Nutrition Enhancement Program (Senegal)
NGO	nongovernmental organization
NSP	National Strategic Plan (Jamaica)
OECD	Organisation for Economic Co-operation and Development
PA	programmatic approaches
PAD	project appraisal document

PDO	project development objective
PMT	project management team
RSR	rapid social response
SABER	Systems Approach for Better Education Results
SAR	South Asia
SIEF	Strategic Impact Evaluation Fund
SIP	Social Inclusion Project (Bulgaria)
SP	social protection sector
SUN	Scaling up Nutrition
SWAp	Sector-Wide Approach
TA	technical assistance
TTL	task team leader
TVET	technical vocational education and training
UN	United Nations
UNESCO	United Nations Educational, Scientific and Cultural Organization
UNICEF	United Nations Children's Fund
USAID	U.S. Agency for International Development
WFP	World Food Programme
WHO	World Health Organization

All dollar amounts are U.S. dollars unless otherwise indicated.

CHAPTER 1

Introduction

Importance of Investing in ECD

Investing in young children is one of the smartest investments that countries can make.[1] Around the world, young children are growing up in disadvantaged circumstances. In developing countries, nearly 40 percent of all children younger than five years are stunted or living in poverty (Grantham-McGregor et al. 2007). These children are more likely to demonstrate lower academic achievement outcomes and exhibit poorer cognitive ability (Glewwe, Jacoby, and King 2001; Vegas and Santibáñez 2010). Disadvantaged children are also less likely to have access to quality health services, basic water and sanitation infrastructure, adequate nutrition, and quality childcare and preschools (Cole and Cole 2000; Grantham-McGregor et al. 2007). These multiple-risk factors can lead to poor physical, socio-emotional, and cognitive development and set children on a path to lower achievement throughout life (Cole and Cole 200; Naudeau 2009). Cross-country evidence shows that by the time children enter primary school, significant gaps exist in children's development; these gaps widen with time. The effects of poor development in early childhood have life-long consequences, setting children on a lower trajectory and adversely impacting a country's social and economic development.

Intervening during early childhood has the potential to mitigate the negative effects of poverty and promote equitable opportunities and better outcomes for education, health, and economic productivity (Heckman 2008a; 2008b; Naudeau et al. 2011). Development in early childhood is a multidimensional and sequential process, with progress in one domain acting as a catalyst for development in other domains (Shonkoff et al. 2012). Interventions to influence a child's development should address four key domains: cognitive development, linguistic development, socio-emotional development, and physical well-being and growth (Naudeau et al. 2011; Vegas and Santibáñez 2010). Entry points to influence these four domains exist in a range of sectors, including health and nutrition, education, and social protection and can be directed toward pregnant women, young children, and parents and caregivers.

As policy makers weigh the costs of investment in early childhood development (ECD), it is becoming increasingly clear that the potential returns far exceed costs. A growing body of literature demonstrates that the returns to investments in children's early years are substantial, particularly when compared to equivalent investments made later in life (Heckman and Masterov 2007). Investments in the early years offer a cost-efficient way to produce a well-trained and capable workforce and lead to better outcomes for those at greatest disadvantage (Naudeau et al. 2011). The benefits to such investments can accrue to individual children and to society more broadly and can be leveraged to influence diverse policy objectives, including improving maternal health, promoting female labor participation, raising additional tax revenue, and reducing expenditures on social assistance programs (for example, Moss 2000). The rate of return on investments to ECD interventions depends on many factors, including the focus, duration of exposure, and quality of programs being implemented, but they have been shown to have benefit-cost ratios as high as 17:1 (Engle et al. 2011). For example, increasing preschool enrollment to 50 percent for children in low- and middle-income countries could result in lifetime earnings gains of US$15–$34 billion. By contrast, failing to ensure high levels of access to ECD services may have significant irreversible damages for individuals and countries in the short-, medium-, and long-term.

Understanding that investing in young children can be a cost-effective strategy to promote a healthier, more productive population, the World Bank has been working for several decades with client governments to invest in ECD policies and programs. The Bank's human development practices support governments in establishing systems that provide essential services in health, nutrition, education, and social protection. The practices have taken a life-cycle step-by-step approach to help countries deliver services that help people live productive lives starting at pregnancy and the earliest years of life (Banerji et al. 2010). The objective is to ensure that all young children are provided opportunities to grow, learn, and develop to their fullest capacity.

This portfolio review builds upon previous portfolio reviews of World Bank investments in young children and youth. In 2001, the World Bank conducted a 10-year review of its ECD project portfolio, which reported that the World Bank had cumulatively lent $1.1 billion to support ECD projects between fiscal years (FY) 1990 and 2000 (Young 2001). This FY 1990 to FY 2000 portfolio review included 13 self-standing ECD operations and 41 ECD components within larger projects. Ten years later, in 2011, the World Bank reviewed investments in children and youth from FY 2000 to FY 2010 (Lefebvre-Hoang and Cunningham 2011). The 2011 report captured a picture of World Bank investments targeted at children and youth aged 0–24 years old. Though an exact comparison between this portfolio review and the earlier reviews by Young (2001) and Lefebvre-Hoang and Cunningham (2011) is not possible because of differences in focus and methodology, it is clear that overall spending on ECD has increased during the past quarter-century.

The study suggests that between 2000 and 2011 the World Bank's investments in ECD managed by the three human development (HD) practices remained relatively stable for both operations and analytical and advisory work. However, in the past two years, the ECD portfolio has substantially grown. This recent increase in ECD investments is related to the recognition of the importance of investing in ECD in development circles, which has really picked up in the last five years. This includes the World Bank's increased priority in ECD, which has been demonstrated through recent policy statements by the three HD practices as well as several recent initiatives that have and will continue to serve as catalysts for expanded investments in the future.

Across the three HD sectors, Health, Nutrition, and Population (HNP), Education (ED), and Social Protection (SP), investments in ECD are supporting efforts to achieve the World Bank's mission to eradicate poverty and boost shared prosperity. A focus on mothers and young children is at the core of the 2007 HNP strategy, which calls for scaling up support for early childhood nutrition, child health, and maternal health services. In addition, *Scaling up Nutrition*, an initiative spearheaded by the World Bank's HNP sector and other development partners, focuses on nutrition in the first 1,000 days. The 2012 SP strategy emphasizes the need to invest in stronger systems to protect the health and well-being of young children. ECD is highlighted as one of the three pillars of the World Bank's 2010–20 education strategy: *Invest early. Invest smartly. Invest for all.* With the vision of achieving "Learning for All," the ED sector prioritizes investing early, recognizing that the foundational skills acquired in early childhood set the stage for a lifetime of learning. In addition to overall sectoral strategies, several important initiatives have catalyzed increased priority in ECD (see chapter 7).

These recent policy statements and initiatives make it clear that there is now higher interest in and increased recognition of the importance of ECD not only at the World Bank but also in the broader development community. In this context, the first objective of this report is to start where the previous ECD portfolio analysis (Young 2001) concluded and provide an analysis of ECD investments through FY 2013, which clearly demonstrate scaled-up investments and higher priority to ECD in recent years. The mapping and analysis of ECD projects in this review helps in providing a synthesis of some of the lessons learned from the activities and investments of the last dozen years in terms of operations and analytical and advisory work.

The study comprises six chapters after this introduction and a brief conclusion. Chapter 2 explains the methodology adopted for the study. Chapter 3 reviews the trend in ECD operations at the World Bank within its ED, HNP, and SP practices. Chapter 4 provides a brief analysis of seven operations that supported ECD through different sectors and types of investments in order to identify what worked well, and some of the challenges encountered. Chapter 5 summarizes lessons learned from the case studies and the overall portfolio review. Chapter 6 reviews the analytical and advisory work done by the World

Bank. Finally, chapter 7 focuses on recent initiatives for expanding ECD investments, discussing both the challenges and recent opportunities for expanding the Bank's ECD portfolio.

Note

1. For a more detailed review, see Neuman and Devercelli (2013) as well as Denboba et al. (2014).

CHAPTER 2

Methodology for the Study

Abstract

Investments in early childhood development (ECD) are needed for children to reach their potential, and they can also bring high returns to countries. The main question asked in this study is to what extent has the World Bank invested in operations and analytical work related to ECD between 2000 and 2013. The study focuses on the experience of its human development practices for Education, Health-Nutrition-Population, and Social Protection-Labor. This chapter outlines the procedure used for the identification of the operations and activities related to ECD reviewed in the study and the methodological choices that were made for data collection and analysis. The chapter starts with a brief discussion of what is meant by ECD and the types of interventions that can be associated with ECD, so that it is clear for the reader what is included in the review, and what is not. The procedure for selecting the activities reviewed (operations plus analytical and advisory work) is then explained in detail.

What Is Meant by ECD and Essential ECD Interventions?

ECD refers to growth and development starting during a woman's pregnancy through her child's entry to primary school. ECD interventions include services for pregnant and lactating mothers, young children, and their families that address the health, nutritional, socio-emotional, cognitive, and linguistic needs during this age period. The exact age span for interventions considered as related to ECD varies depending on the analyst or country. For this study, ECD is considered as covering the period from pregnancy to the entry in primary school.

ECD interventions therefore include services for pregnant and lactating mothers, as well as young children and their families. Box 2.1 defines ECD and summarizes the types of interventions for early childhood. These services are meant to address the health, nutritional, socio-emotional, cognitive, and linguistic needs during this age period. They are essential because a child's early life forms the basis for future learning, good health, and well-being, as well as the ability of the child to work well with others in adulthood.

Box 2.1 Clarifying the Definition of ECD and Related Terms

There are variations in the exact definition of early childhood development between organizations, academics, and practitioners. In addition, the terms used by countries for interventions that address ECD vary, depending on the focus of the country's policies, interventions, and the local terminology. Terms used to reference early childhood education interventions can include early childhood care and development (ECCD), early childhood education (ECE), or early childhood care and education (ECCE), for example. In addition, maternal and child health or nutrition interventions are not necessarily termed ECD interventions, though they are designed to promote early childhood development.

For the purposes of this portfolio review, we are using the following definition of early childhood development (ECD): The period from when a child is conceived to 83 months of age (until the child reaches the age of seven). ECD addresses children's basic needs in health, nutrition, cognitive, and social-emotional development. Effective ECD policies and interventions reach infants, toddlers, and children including the transition to school entry, as well as pregnant women, parents, and caregivers.

The human development (HD) portfolio reviewed in this document includes a variety of interventions across sectors that promote ECD, including the following:

- **Early childhood care and education (ECCE):** This includes care (typically for children ages 0–24 months) and education (typically for children ages 24–83 months). Quality programs address both care and education for these age groups.
- **Preschool/preprimary/early childhood education (ECE):** This includes interventions that provide opportunities for children to interact with responsive adults and actively learn with peers to prepare for primary school entry; this generally refers to interventions for children ages 36–83 months of age.
- **Early stimulation:** This includes opportunities for young children to interact with caring adults and to learn about the environment from the earliest age; this generally refers to interventions for children ages 0–24 months and to programs designed to teach parents how to engage in early stimulation activities with young children.
- **Early childhood health interventions:** This includes initiatives in health care, including health service provision, disease prevention, and health promotion to provide the continuum of maternal and child pre- and postnatal care. Services include standard health screenings for pregnant women, skilled attendants at delivery, childhood immunizations, and well-child visits.
- **Early childhood nutrition interventions:** This includes initiatives to ensure that pregnant women, breastfeeding mothers, and young children are adequately nourished. Interventions may include breastfeeding promotion, responsible and appropriate complementary feeding, dietary diversity, salt iodization, and micro-nutrient supplementation.
- **Child and social protection interventions:** This includes initiatives targeted to protect the well-being of children by supporting the extremely poor and vulnerable (social protection) or focusing on measures to prevent and respond to abuse, neglect, exploitation, and vio-

box continues next page

Box 2.1 Clarifying the Definition of ECD and Related Terms *(continued)*

lence affecting children (child protection). Interventions can protect children in marginalized communities and those who are excluded due to gender, disability, human immunodeficiency virus/acquired immune deficiency syndrome (HIV/AIDS), or other sociocultural factors. Services may include birth registration, tracking and preventing child abuse, cash and in-kind transfer programs, and parenting programs to promote positive caregiving.
- *Integrated ECD services:* This includes multidimensional services combined to comprehensively meet an array of child development needs, combining the types of sectoral interventions described above to promote a child's health, nutrition, cognitive development, social development, and protection.

What Has Been Included in This Review and What Has Not?

The previous section makes it clear that a comprehensive ECD strategy involves many different types of interventions and services, as well as support to the institutions providing those services. This makes the identification of the universe of ECD interventions complex in part because many different projects not directly focused on ECD may still have ECD components.

In its project database warehouse the World Bank does not have a sector or thematic code that identifies ECD projects. There is no easy way through an automatic procedure to capture automatically Bank investments supporting ECD. But the Bank databases can be used to search for some of the most relevant thematic codes related to ECD projects that are often used to categorize projects. These terms would include, for example, the "pre-primary education" sector code, the "child health" thematic code, and the "nutrition and food security" thematic code. One needs to be careful however because these codes may include projects that are not ECD specific and they may also exclude other projects that have ECD components.

In order to track the Bank's investments specifically for ECD in a consistent and comprehensive manner, the procedure followed focused only on investments across the portfolios of the three HD practices. That is, the focus was on investments managed by one of the three practices for Education (ED), Health-Nutrition-Population (HNP), and Social Protection-Labor (SP), but not investments by other practices that may relate to ECD. The types of projects and tasks included in the search belonged to two different groups:

- *Operations* are projects funded by loans or grants given directly to client countries for implementation of ECD interventions or for improvement of country systems related to ECD. These include International Bank for Reconstruction and Development/International Development Association (IBRD/IDA) operations as well as trust-funded operations, but the bulk of the funding commitments made takes place through IBRD/IDA operations.

- *Analytical, Advisory, and Partnership Activities*[1] are tasks that create and use knowledge (and in some cases partnerships) to help improve the effectiveness of the Bank's work as well as country systems, policies, and programs. These include principally economic and sector work (ESW), technical assistance (TA), knowledge products (KP), impact evaluations (IE), and global partnerships and programs (GPP).

Due to the diversity of projects and tasks targeting young children, all project documents related to the three practices were manually reviewed and additional inputs from colleagues in the three sectors were also gathered. In a systematic way, the following steps were followed to generate a comprehensive database of World Bank HD projects and activities on ECD:

1. *Keyword search to identify potential projects of interest.* Using keyword searches in the Bank's Operations Portal and E-Trust Funds portal for all 3,681 HD operations and activities that were approved between FY 2001 and FY 2013, a preliminary list of 2,016 HD projects was generated. We used a comparable keyword search methodology as done for other portfolio reviews at the World Bank, including a child and youth portfolio review (Lefebvre-Hoang and Cunningham 2011), but we focused only on keywords related to early childhood (0–83 months) within HD. We excluded youth-specific keywords and only searched within the three HD sectors. The keywords used included "child(ren)," "ECD," "maternal," "nutrition," "orphan," "child health," and "preprimary." To ensure we captured all relevant projects in the databases, we included additional sector-specific keywords, based on the Systems Approach for Better Education Results-Early Childhood Development (SABER-ECD) indicators (the SABER-ECD program is described in chapter 5 of this study). These keywords included the following: "Antenatal," "birth attendant," "birth registration," "breastfeeding," "child immunizations," "child protection," "child safety net," "complementary feeding," "continued feeding," "early childhood," "infant," "iron fortification," "maternal," "newborn," "oral rehydration," "orphans," "parenting," "prenatal," "preprimary," "preschool," "salt iodization," "vitamin A supplementation," "vulnerable children," and "young children."
2. *Manual review of project documents.* Project documents were manually reviewed to gather information about each project. Documents reviewed include Project Appraisal Documents (PADs), Implementation Completion Results (ICR) Reports, Implementation Status and Results (ISR) reports, Program Documents, and/or Project Papers.
3. *Filter list to projects with specific ECD activities.* Upon reviewing the details of each operation or activity, each one was categorize as (i) self-standing, (ii) component or subcomponent, or (iii) likely to benefit young children (with no explicit investment in ECD). Approximately half of the projects generated through the preliminary keyword search were not added to the database because they did not specifically support ECD.

Methodology for the Study

4. ***ECD costs calculated.*** When estimating funding for ECD projects and activities, investments committed specifically to ECD were calculated from the information available in the project documents. For components, only component cost was included in our estimate of the Bank's investment in ECD. In many cases, Bank funding for ECD components was listed clearly in project documents. However, in instances where only total ECD component costs were listed (and not Bank funding per component), the Bank commitment was calculated as the same proportion of Bank commitment to the total project cost. For example, if IDA contributed a total of $7.5 million and the total project cost was $10 million and the total component cost was $1 million, then the Bank commitment to ECD is estimated as $750,000.

Figure 2.1 visualizes the approach used for reviewing and filtering projects. Upon compiling the list of the 273 activities with explicit investments in ECD in the World Bank's HD portfolio from FY 2001 to FY 2013, an analysis of trends in commitments and number of projects was completed. In addition to the direct investments, 232 projects were identified that did not explicitly focus on ECD but were likely to benefit young children. These projects include 152 projects in HNP, 59 projects in SP, and 21 projects in ED. Examples of areas of focus included health sector reforms resulting in improved maternal and child health

Figure 2.1 Selection of Projects for This Review

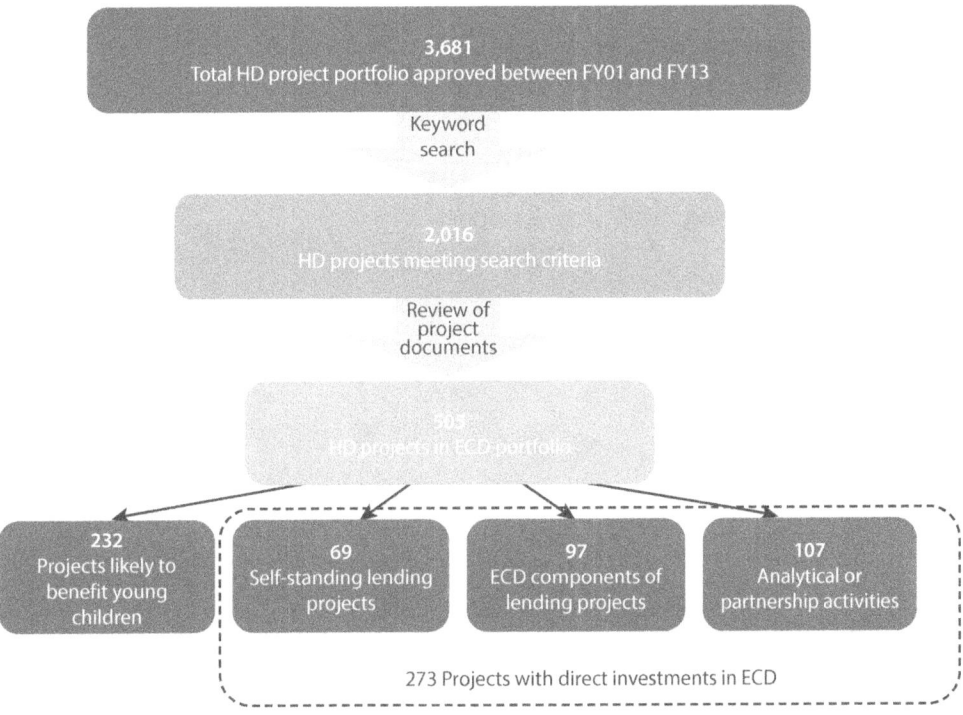

Source: World Bank data.
Note: ECD = early childhood development; HD = human development.

services, HIV/AIDS interventions including the prevention of mother-to-child transmission, safety net projects targeted towards poor mothers to address food insecurity, or education sector reforms designed to improve basic education, including preschool (but with no direct investment in a preschool component). While these 232 projects in all likelihood resulted in significant benefits for young children, they were not included in the detailed analysis of the 273 activities and operations explicitly focused on ECD.

It is also important to emphasize that whole areas benefitting young children were also excluded from the analysis because of its focus on investments managed by the three human development practices for education (ED), health-nutrition-population (HNP), and social protection (SP)-labor sectors. The present portfolio does not include operations related to other sectors such as agriculture and water and sanitation, even though children are among their main beneficiaries.

Finally, in order to better understand how well ECD projects have been designed and implemented by the World Bank, a more detailed analysis of seven operations from the portfolio was conducted. World Bank staff from the ECD Community of Practice selected examples of operations that have valuable lessons of challenges and opportunities in implementing ECD operations. To gain an understanding of the diversity of context and stages of implementation, the selected cases include both closed and active lending operations from across the six World Bank regions and three HD sectors. These case studies focused on trust-funded or IBRD/IDA operations (loans and grants), although some included analytical work as well.

In preparing these cases studies, ICR reports (for closed operations), ISR reports (for active operations), PADs, and associated research and articles on specific projects were reviewed. Additionally, task team leaders (TTLs) and other World Bank staff involved in the specific operations were interviewed to gain a first-hand perspective on the operations.

Note

1. We did not include training in the portfolio review.

CHAPTER 3

Trends in Operations

Abstract

This chapter reviews trends in the World Bank's operations related to early childhood development (ECD) over the period FY 2001 to FY 2013. The focus is on International Bank for Reconstruction and Development/International Development Association (IBRD/IDA) operations within the education, health-nutrition-population, and social protection portfolio. A total of 116 operations with ECD components were implemented between FY 2001 and FY 2013 with total commitments of $3.4 billion (in US$ of 2013). The number of operations and the funding committed remained relatively stable from FY 2001 to FY 2011, but increased substantially in the last two years. This increase aligns with the adoption of a series of policy statements over the last few years on the importance of ECD by the World Bank. ECD investments per person (or per person in poverty) were larger in countries with higher levels of gross domestic product (GDP) per capita, suggesting lower absorption capacity or demand, or at least a less extensive tradition of ECD operations in low-income countries. Investments were also larger in health than in education and social protection.

IBRD/IDA Operations: Commitment Levels and Trends

In real terms, the World Bank's human development (HD) sectors invested $3.4 billion between FY 2001 and FY 2013 through 116 operations funded by loans and grants. Over the past 13 years, 39 ECD operations were funded by International Bank for Reconstruction and Development (IBRD) loans and 77 were funded by International Development Association (IDA) grants. Total IBRD/IDA commitments between FY 2001 and FY 2013 amount to $3.1 billion in nominal terms, and $3.4 billion in US$ of 2013. Although this is often not done in portfolio reviews, it is important to assess trends in real terms, given that the cumulative impact of inflation for the period as a whole is at close to 30 percent. In other words, inflation by itself would generate an apparent increase in commitments of close to 30 percent between FY 2001 and FY 2013, but this would not represent an increase in resources, given the rise in the cost of living

Table 3.1 Trend in the Number of IBRD/IDA Operations and Funding for ECD

FY	Number of HD ECD operations	Lending and grants for ECD, nominal terms (US$ million)	Adjustment factor from US GDP deflator[a]	Lending and grants, 2013 real terms (US$ million)	Average amount per operation (US$ million)
FY01	8	154.9	82.9	197.7	24.7
FY02	9	97.4	84.4	122.2	13.6
FY03	10	146.9	85.9	181.0	18.1
FY04	4	127.3	87.8	153.4	38.3
FY05	8	136.9	90.5	160.2	20.0
FY06	7	322.1	93.5	364.6	52.1
FY07	5	265.0	96.2	291.6	58.3
FY08	12	114.9	98.2	123.8	10.3
FY09	10	158.2	99.9	167.7	16.8
FY10	7	220.3	100.4	232.3	33.2
FY11	9	184.0	102.2	190.6	21.2
FY12	12	465.1	104.1	472.8	39.4
FY13	15	694.4	105.8	694.4	46.3
Total	116	3,087.5	n.a.	3,352.2	n.a.
Average per year	8.9	237.5	n.a.	257.9	30.2

Source: World Bank data.
Note: ECD = early childhood development; FY = fiscal year; GDP = gross domestic product; HD = human development; IBRD = International Bank for Reconstruction and Development; IDA = International Development Association; n.a. = not applicable.
a. Adjustment based on average of quarterly US GDP Implicit Price Deflator for each fiscal year. (US Department of Commerce: Bureau of Economic Analysis).

in beneficiary countries. For simplicity, the US GDP deflator was used to transform nominal commitments into commitments in real terms.

Table 3.1 displays the number of IBRD/IDA operations and the corresponding financial commitments to ECD by fiscal year of approval. The Bank invested an average of nine operations per year, with an average of $258 million per year in commitments (US$ of 2013). The IBRD/IDA portfolio includes 33 self-standing ECD operations, which have an average cost of $45.7 million and 83 ECD components or subcomponents within larger operations, which have an average cost of $22.5 million.

Support to ECD within the HD sectors remained relatively flat from FY 2001 to FY 2011 but increased substantially in FY 2012 and FY 2013. Figure 3.1 displays ECD lending and grant commitments between FY 2001 and FY 2013. Overall investments have increased from $198 million (US$ of 2013) in 2001 to $694.4 in 2013. Spikes in spending in FY 2006 and FY 2007 are associated with a handful of large operations implemented in these two years. These include: a $243 million IBRD loan for the Argentine Ministry of Health to implement a Maternal and Child Health Insurance Program in order to reduce infant mortality rates; a $104 million component of an IDA grant to the Ministry of

Figure 3.1 IBRD/IDA ECD Operations in the HD Portfolio, US$ million (US$ of 2013)

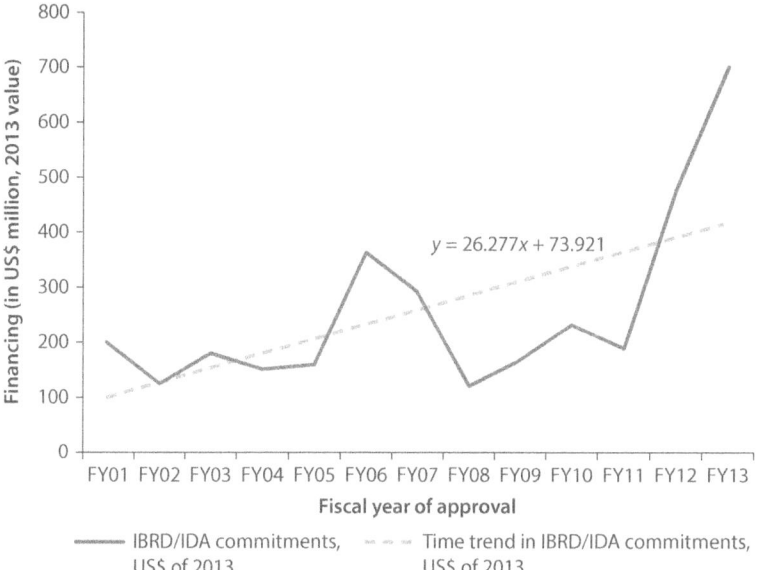

Source: World Bank data.
Note: ECD = early childhood development; HD = human development; IBRD = International Bank for Reconstruction and Development; IDA = International Development Association.

Health of the Democratic Republic of Congo to expand access to essential health services, including vaccinations, vitamin A supplementation, distribution of insecticide-treated bed nets (ITNs), neonatal health services, and Integrated Management of Childhood Illnesses; and a $92 million IDA credit to the Ministry of Education in Indonesia to develop a community-based early childhood education and development project in FY 2007.

In the first 11 years of the observed portfolio, except for the peak observed in FY 2006 and FY 2007, commitments have remained somewhat stable. However, investments have dramatically increased since 2011, with $473 million invested in FY 2012 and $694 invested in FY 2013. This is visualized in figure 3.1 through the line of best fit for the trend in commitments for FY 2001–FY 2013. The line of best fit clearly suggests an increase over time in commitments.

Figure 3.2 displays the number of ECD operations each year, which have increased overall from 8 in FY 2001 to 15 in FY 2013, but have fluctuated each year. Similar to the spending trend displayed in figure 3.1, the number of ECD operations demonstrates an upward trend in FY 2012 to FY 2013. Between FY 2001 and FY 2011, the HD practices approved an average of eight ECD operations per year, compared to an average of 14 operations per year between FY 2012 and FY 2013.

The increase of ECD IBRD/IDA investments in recent years may be partially attributed to sectoral policy statements made by the World Bank on the importance of ECD in recent years. In 2010, through Scaling up Nutrition (SUN) initiative, the World Bank, along with international partners including the European Commission, the United Nations (UN) Standing Committee on Nutrition, U.S.

Figure 3.2 IBRD/IDA ECD Operations in the HD Portfolio, Number

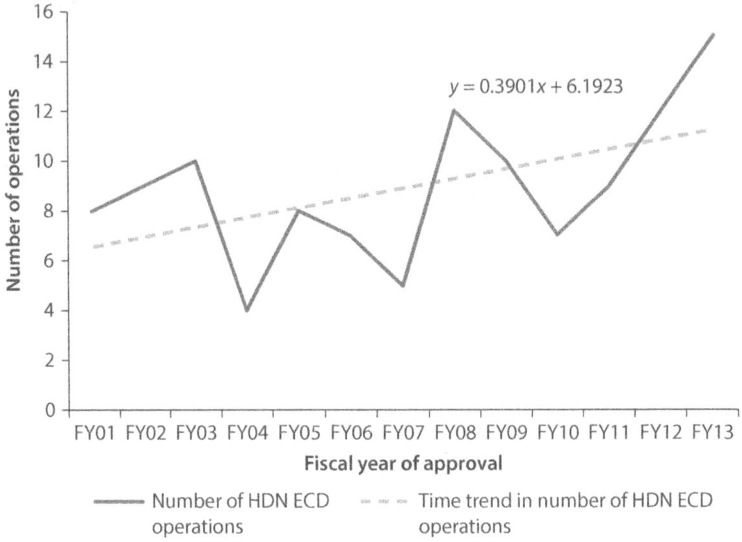

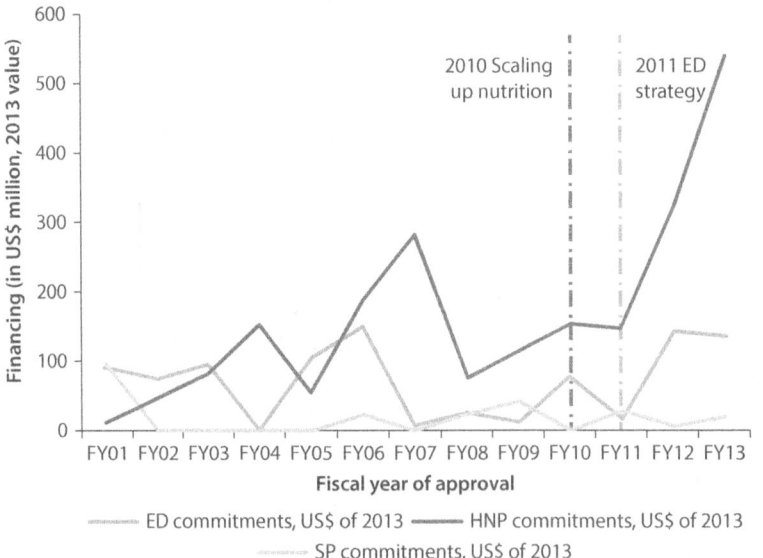

$y = 0.3901x + 6.1923$

Source: World Bank data.
Note: ECD = early childhood development; HD = human development; HDN = Human Development Network; IBRD = International Bank for Reconstruction and Development; IDA = International Development Association.

Figure 3.3 IBRD/IDA ECD Operations in ED, HNP, and SP US$ million (US$ of 2013)

Source: World Bank data.
Note: ED = education sector; HNP = health, nutrition, and population sector; IBRD = International Bank for Reconstruction and Development; IDA = International Development Association; SP = social protection sector.

Agency for International Development (USAID), World Food Programme (WFP), and World Health Organization (WHO) set forth priorities for action to address undernutrition. As displayed in figure 3.3, health, nutrition, and population (HNP) investments have dramatically increased since the SUN initiative was launched. In 2011, the Bank's education department put forth its Education Strategy 2020, *Learning for All*, where investing early is one of the top three priorities. As displayed in figure 3.3, since the 2011 release of the strategy, ECD operations in education have increased. The new social protection strategy adopted in 2012 emphasizes the need to invest in stronger systems to protect the health and well-being of young children. Social protection (SP) sector IBRD/IDA operations have not yet increased, but in the next few years, this trend can be reassessed.

Overall ECD spending increased during the last decade as compared to the previous one. Compared to previous estimates of ECD spending, the World Bank has invested more. In 2001, a 10-year review of the Bank's children and youth project portfolio reported that the World Bank had cumulatively lent $1.1 billion to support ECD projects between FY 1990 and FY 2000 (Young 2001). This review included 13 self-standing ECD operations and 41 ECD components within larger projects. Although an exact comparison between this portfolio review and the earlier reviews by Young (2001) and Lefebvre-Hoang and Cunningham (2011) is not possible because of differences in focus and methodology, it appears that overall spending on ECD increased during the last decade as compared to the previous one, even after accounting for inflation. The previous review suggested that nearly 50 percent of ECD projects were in Latin America and the Caribbean and approximately 25 percent in Africa. In this study, as shown above, these remained the two regions with the largest investments in ECD.

IBRD/IDA Commitments by Sector, Region, and Country Income

Among the three HD sectors, commitments to ECD were largest in the HNP sector. As shown in table 3.2, the largest commitments to ECD were made in the HNP sector, which invested $2.2 billion, representing nearly two-thirds of the full HD IBRD/IDA ECD portfolio. ED invested $935 million through 42 projects and SP invested $241million through 15 projects. HNP operations tended to be larger investments, with an average commitment of $37 million per project. This is compared to an average $22 million per ED project and an average $16 million per SP project.

The region that benefitted from the largest HD ECD commitments was Latin America and the Caribbean, followed by Sub-Saharan Africa. In the past 13 years, Latin America and the Caribbean and Africa each had 37 IBRD/IDA ECD projects, with total commitments of $1.3 billion in Latin America and the Caribbean and $1.1 billion in Africa. A total of 61 countries received funding from IBRD or IDA over the 13-year period. Map 3.1 displays the distribution of HD IBRD/IDA ECD projects between FY 2001 and FY 2013.

World Bank ECD investments per child tended to be higher in middle-income countries. The fact that middle-income regions (and thereby countries) such as Latin America and the Caribbean benefitted from larger commitments to ECD in the HD portfolio than other regions can also be illustrated using a

Table 3.2 IBRD/IDA Commitments (in US$ of 2013) to ECD by Region and Sector

	Education		Health, nutrition and population		Social protection		All three sectors	
	Number of projects	Commitments (US$ millions)	Number of projects	Commitments (US$ millions)	Number of projects	Commitments (US$ millions)	Number of projects	Commitments (US$ millions)
Africa	9	142.8	25	982.9	3	9.4	37	1,145.6
East Asia and Pacific	2	205.1	3	8.8	0	0.0	5	213.8
Europe and Central Asia	4	19.1	3	28.5	2	51.0	9	98.6
Latin America and the Caribbean	19	484.0	11	686.5	7	161.0	37	1,331.5
Middle East and North Africa	5	64.6	5	73.1	2	3.8	12	141.5
South Asia	3	9.6	12	396.0	1	16.0	16	421.6
All	42	935.2	59	2,175.9	15	241.2	116	3,352.2

Source: World Bank data.
Note: ECD = early childhood development; IBRD = International Bank for Reconstruction and Development; IDA = International Development Association.

Map 3.1 Global Distribution of HD ECD Investments through IBRD/IDA

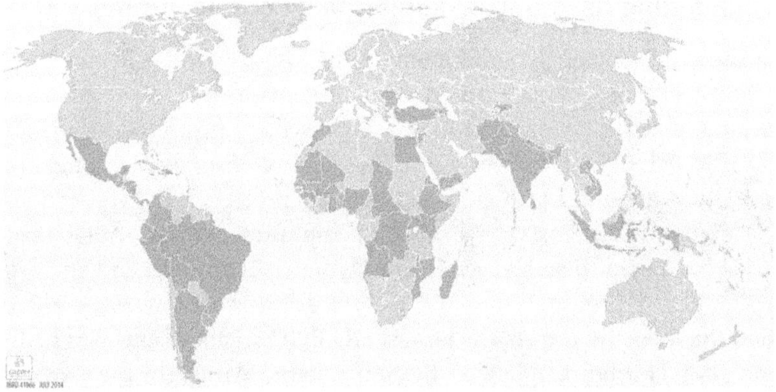

Source: World Bank data.

simple scatter plot of the amount invested in ECD over the period as a whole in any given country per person. This is done in figure 3.4 where the horizontal axis represents the purchasing power parity GDP per capita level for countries that benefitted from ECD investments and the vertical axis represents the IBRD/IDA amount invested in ECD per child under the age of five in the country throughout the 13-year period from FY 2001 to FY 2013. The size of the bubbles in the figure is proportional to the amount of total IBRD/IDA funding received by each

Figure 3.4 IBRD/IDA Investment in ECD in the HD Portfolio Per Child under Five

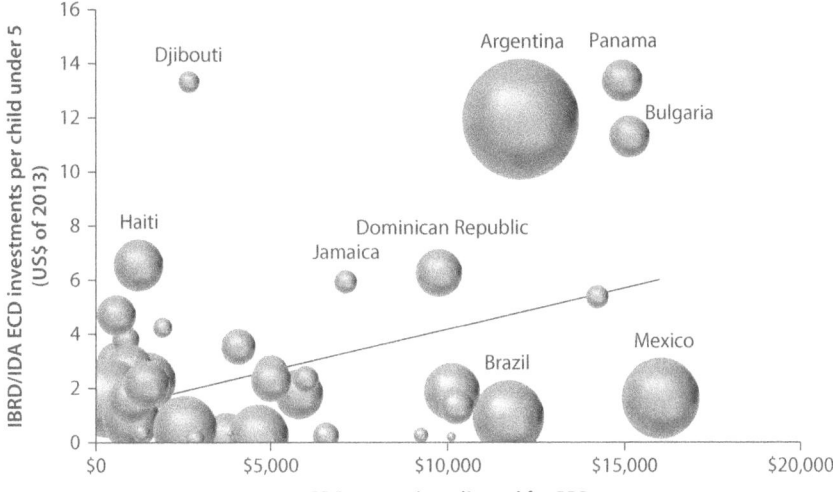

Source: World Bank data.
Note: Size of data point = total IBRD/IDA ECD spending in that country. ECD = early childhood development; GDP = gross domestic product; HD = human development; IBRD = International Bank for Reconstruction and Development; IDA = International Development Association; PPP = purchasing power parity.

country. Detailed data on commitments per country, per person, and per poor person are provided in table A.1 in appendix A. Additionally, figure A.1 in appendix A displays the distribution of HD IBRD/IDA ECD commitments per child under five.

There is an upward trend in the amounts invested per person as a function of the level of GDP per capita in the countries. The largest investments were among Latin American countries with the highest level of GDP per capita. Argentina benefited from the largest investments ($448 million over the period, in real terms); the third largest investments occurred in Mexico ($203 million in real terms), although due to its larger population, the amount invested per person in Mexico was smaller; and Brazil benefited from $158 million (real terms).

However, low-income countries also benefitted from large overall investments. The Democratic Republic of Congo (DRC), Ethiopia, Afghanistan, Haiti, Malawi, Mozambique, and Nepal are among the top quintile of countries with the largest overall ECD investments, yet are each in the lowest quintile of GDP per capita. For example, the second largest investment was for the DRC ($208 million, in real terms). Overall, when countries are ranked according to the investments in ECD per person in the HD IBRD/IDA portfolio, many of the countries with the highest investments per person are middle income countries. When looking at investments per person in poverty according to the benchmark poverty line of $1.25 per person per day, the gaps in investments between higher- and lower-income countries are even larger.

Thus, in part because middle-income countries have had a longer tradition of investing in ECD and also have a higher absorption capacity for ECD investments due to the fact that they already have existing delivery systems, they have tended to benefit from larger ECD investments over the period as a whole (apart from absorptive capacity, other factors could play a role in the difference in ECD investments according to the level of income per capita of countries).

ECD investments per child under five are relatively small. The ratio of total IBRD/IDA commitments to the under-5 population in each country range from a maximum of $13.44 per person per year in Panama to $0.03 in Kenya. Some of these amounts are much higher when considering investments per poor person, but this is in large part because the definition of poverty is based on the international benchmark of $1.25 per person per day, and this is a low benchmark for middle-income countries, so using this benchmark overstates the investments likely to be obtained by the poor assuming targeting of the interventions to them (in middle-income countries, the investments do not target, say, the poorest 1 percent of the population, and even if they tried, they would probably not be successful in doing so).

ECD Share in Human Development IBRD/IDA Operations

The period from FY 2001 to FY 2013 was not homogenous in terms of economic conditions in developing countries. The first few years witnessed high rates of economic growth in many countries, while as of FY 2008 the period was characterized by a severe recession in Organisation for Economic Co-operation and Development (OECD) countries which led to downturns in many developing countries as well. During that period lending related to human development, and especially to safety nets, increased substantially, which led to a decline in the share of ECD lending in the human development portfolio, as was shown in table 3.1 and figure 3.1.

Specifically, as a share of the overall HD commitments, the proportion allocated to ECD decreased after a peak in FY 2006 of 5.5 percent to an average of just above 2 percent in the last three years from FY 2009 to FY 2011. But after the recession, as overall commitments to HD operations receded from their peak during the crisis, and as the ECD portfolio increased substantially, the share of the commitments allocated to ECD also grew. Overall, for the period as a whole, there has been a clear increase in the share of the HD portfolio allocated to ECD, as shown in figure 3.5.

Table 3.3 provides more detailed information by giving the average number of projects and commitments for the HD and ECD portfolios over the period as a whole, as well as for the first eight years (FY 2001 to FY 2008), the period of the crisis (FY 2009 to FY 2011), and the last two years. Over the period as a whole, a total of 1,161 IBRD/IDA operations were approved for education, health, and social protection. As mentioned earlier, 116 of these operations were focused on ECD or included an ECD component. ECD was thus included in 10 percent of all IBRD/IDA HD operations and it represented 4.3 percent of commitments over the period as a whole. If one compares the average share of the HD portfolio

Figure 3.5 Share of ECD Commitments in Overall HD Portfolio

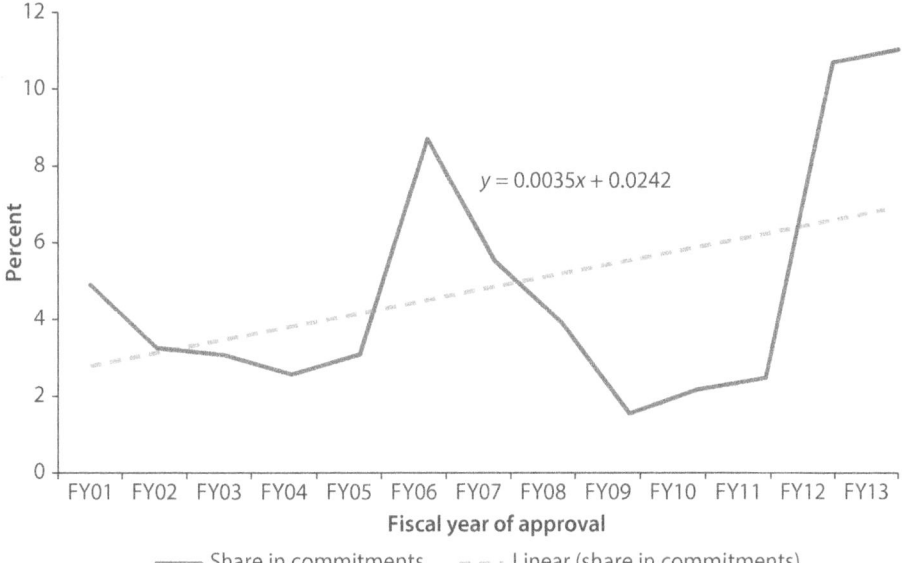

Source: World Bank data.
Note: ECD = early childhood development; HD = human development.

Table 3.3 Share of ECD in HD IBRD/IDA Portfolio by Time Period

	ECD			HD			Shares	
	Number of projects	Total amount ($M)	Average amount ($M)	Number of projects	Total amount ($M)	Average amount ($M)	Share of funding (%)	Share of projects (%)
All years	116.0	3,083.8	237.2	1,161.0	69,887.8	5,376.0	4.4	10.0
FY01–08	63.0	1,361.7	170.2	617.0	31,590.3	3,948.8	4.3	10.2
FY09–11	26.0	562.6	187.5	321.0	27,674.4	9,224.8	2.0	8.1
FY12–13	27.0	1,159.5	579.8	223.0	10,623.1	5,311.6	10.9	12.1

Source: World Bank data.
Note: ECD = early childhood development; HD = human development; IBRD = International Bank for Reconstruction and Development; IDA = International Development Association.

allocated to ECD over the period from FY 2001 to FY 2008 to the share of the crisis years and finally the last two years, the decrease from the first eight years to the crisis years was from 4.4 percent to 2.0 percent, but the share increased dramatically to 10.9 percent in the last two years.

In terms of amounts, between the first and second periods, commitments to ECD increased slightly from $170.2 million annually during FY 2001 to FY 2008 to $187.5 million annually during FY 2009 to FY 2011. This small increase was observed thanks in part to a larger number of projects with an ECD component in the last three years versus the first eight. The number of HD projects during

FY 2009 to FY 2011 also increased versus the average for the first eight years. But the main difference was that in FY 2009 to FY 2011, the average size of the HD projects increased substantially (it almost doubled). In the last two years after the crisis, both the number of ECD projects and the size of those projects increased, leading to a jump in commitments to $579.8 million per year.

Trust-Funded ECD Operations

In addition to IBRD/IDA operations, 50 ECD operations were funded through $217 million in trust funds. These operations include recipient-executed operations and special finance operations for emergency situations. These operations are smaller than IBRD/IDA projects, with average budgets of $4.3 million per operation. Table 3.4 presents the number and corresponding commitments of trust-funded projects by region and sector. The Africa region had significantly more trust-funded ECD operations than any other region, committing $132 million in trust funds between FY 2001 and FY 2013. HNP has the greatest financial commitments ($123 million) and ED had a greatest number of projects (27 projects).

Figure 3.6 displays the financial commitments to ECD through trust-funded operations in HD between FY 2001 and FY 2013. In the first 10 years, the majority of ECD trust-funded operations occurred between FY 2007 and FY 2011 in part because more trust funds were available in that period. Between FY 2009 and FY 2012, commitments dramatically rose (but fell again in FY 2013). Eighteen of these operations were funded by Fast-Track Initiative (FTI) which, in

Table 3.4 Trust-funded Operations (in US$ of 2013) to ECD by Region and Sector

	Education		Health, nutrition, and population		Social protection		All three sectors	
	Number of projects	Commitments (US$ millions)	Number of projects	Commitments (US$ millions)	Number of projects	Commitments (US$ millions)	Number of projects	Commitments (US$ millions)
Africa	17	37.1	8	90.5	2	4.6	27	132.2
East Asia and Pacific	6	31.5	3	4.3	0	0.0	9	35.9
Europe and Central Asia	3	13.4	3	16.9	0	0.0	6	30.2
Latin America and the Caribbean	1	2.8	1	0.2	3	4.7	5	7.7
Middle East and North Africa	0	0.0	2	10.4	0	0.0	2	10.4
South Asia	0	0.0	1	0.5	0	0.0	1	0.5
All	27	84.8	18	122.7	5	9.3	50	216.8

Source: World Bank data.
Note: ECD = early childhood development.

Figure 3.6 Trust-funded ECD Operations in the HD Portfolio, US$ million (US$ of 2013)

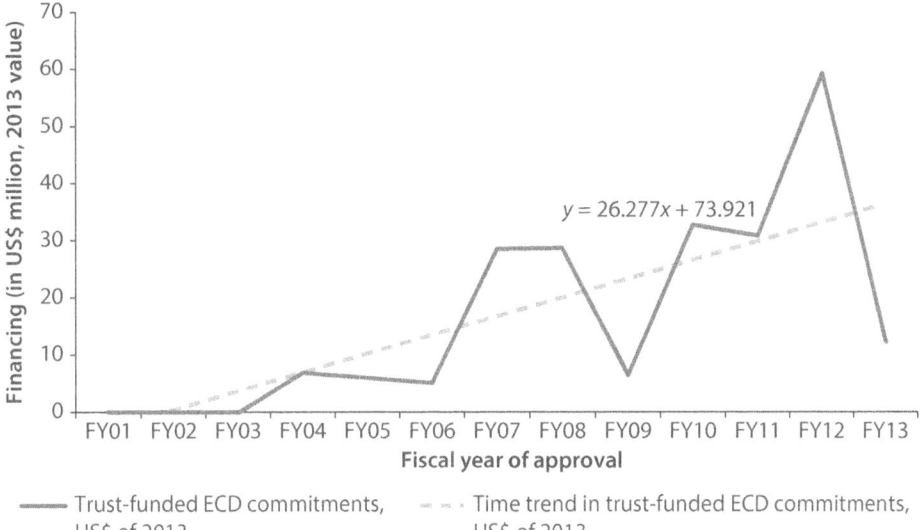

Source: World Bank data.
Note: ECD = early childhood development; HD = human development.

September, 2011, officially became the Global Partnership for Education (GPE), which also actively supports ECD. In 2012, for example, a $10 million GPE grant for the Mongolia Global Partnership for Education Early Childhood Education (GPE ECE) Project aimed to improve access to ECE for children in disadvantaged communities. Other sources of trust funding included among others the Rapid Social Response (RSR), the Japan Social Development Fund (JSDF), the Global Food Crisis Response Program (GFCR), the Global Partnership on Output-based Aid (GPBA), the Africa Catalytic Growth Fund (ACGF), the Netherlands Partnership Program (DUTCHP), and the Food Price Crisis Response (FPCR).

Operations Likely to Benefit Children

As explained in chapter 2, this report and the estimates provided above are based on a list of 273 activities with explicit investments in ECD in the World Bank's HD portfolio from FY 2001 to FY 2013. But we also found 232 other operations (loans, grants, and trust funded) which, while not explicitly focusing on ECD, were nevertheless likely to benefit young children. These projects include 152 projects in HNP, 59 projects in SP, and 21 projects in ED. These 232 projects were not included in the analysis, but the complete list and total commitments are provided in appendix B.

One example of support for safety nets during the crisis was the World Bank's funding for the Brazilian government's *Bolsa Familia (BF)* social welfare program that helps and incentivizes poor families to access health, education, and other services. In 2010, the World Bank committed $200 million for a second adaptable program loan to expand the program. The project's development objective was to "strengthen the BF Program's ability to achieve its objective of reducing poverty and inequity and promoting human capital development by improving schooling and health status of children and reducing incidence of malnutrition among the poor population." The loan was designed to consolidate the safety net program, improve the targeting system, strengthen monitoring and evaluation, and identify ways to link beneficiaries to complementary services. While the project did not have any direct financing specifically for ECD-aged children, it is likely to have provided benefits to young children through support to vulnerable families. In addition to receiving income support, which can allow families to invest in their children's basic needs (evidence suggests that most of the money is used to buy food, school supplies, and clothes for children), project beneficiary households were required to take steps related to ECD interventions, such as ensuring that their children get immunized and that they also maintain regular visits to health clinics.

Another example implemented before the great recession was support for the Malawi Third Social Action Fund. In 2003, the World Bank partnered with the Government of Malawi (GoM) to support the Community Empowerment and Development Program. The Third Social Action Fund aimed to continue public interventions that promoted sustainable poverty reduction at the community level. The project development objective was to "empower individuals, households, communities, and their development partners in the implementation of measures which can assist them in better managing risks associated with health, education, sanitation, water, transportation, energy, and food insecurity, and to provide support to the critically vulnerable through a variety of sustainable interventions." The project focused on poor communities with inadequate access to social services (such as schools, clinics, water, and effective transportation). It included five components: (i) community development projects based on community service packages of health, education, transport and communication, food security, and water and sanitation; (ii) social support program targeted toward vulnerable groups including the elderly, orphans and foster parents, destitute, disabled, persons affected by human immunodeficiency virus/acquired immune deficiency syndrome (HIV/AIDs), and malnourished children under five; (iii) community savings and investment promotion; (iv) transparency and accountability promotion; and (v) institutional development. While the project did not allocate specific financing to young children, it serves as an example of a social protection intervention that empowered disadvantaged families to break the cycle of poverty and disadvantage.

CHAPTER 4

Case Studies of Operations

Abstract

In order to gain a deeper understanding of the design, implementation, and results of some of the World Bank's early childhood development (ECD) operations, this chapter provides an analysis of seven ECD operations. Information was collected via a review of project documents and personal interviews with the task team leaders (TTL) and other Bank staff involved in the operations. The cases were purposely selected to vary by region, level of development of the countries' ECD systems, and sectoral focus in order to capture diverse experiences. This chapter presents key findings for each of the case studies, while the following chapter presents lessons learned, including common challenges, as well as features of successful ECD projects.

Selection of the Case Studies

This chapter presents a brief analysis of seven ECD operations approved between FY 2001 and FY 2011. The objective is to gain an understanding of what worked well, or in some cases required improvements, in terms of design and implementation. The operations were selected on the basis of conversation with World Bank staffs from the education sector (ED), health, nutrition, and population (HNP) sector, and social protection (SP) sector practices, with the aim to identify examples of operations that could provide valuable lessons in terms of both challenges and opportunities. On purpose, the selection of operations covers various stages of implementation (some operations are now closed while others are still active) as well as all of the six World Bank regions and the three human development sectors or practices. The selected operations were mostly funded through International Bank for Reconstruction and Development (IBRD) and International Development Association (IDA), but some benefited from trust funds. Most of the operations are substantial in size but not necessarily the largest ones.

The seven case studies selected were the Bulgaria social inclusion project, the Eritrea integrated early childhood development project, the Indonesia early childhood education and development project, the Jamaica early childhood

Table 4.1 Summary of ECD Case Studies

Country and project	Duration	Bank contribution to ECD (in nominal US$)	Total project cost (in nominal US$)	Target population (end target, not necessarily number of beneficiaries reached)	Project development objective
BULGARIA: *SOCIAL INCLUSION PROJECT*	FY09–FY16	43 million (IBRD loan)	43 million	15,000 children below the age of seven and their parents from low-income and marginalized families	To promote social inclusion through increasing the school readiness of children below the age of seven, targeting low-income and marginalized families (including children with a disability and other special needs).
ERITREA: *INTEGRATED EARLY CHILDHOOD DEVELOPMENT PROJECT*	FY01–FY07	40 million (IDA credit)	49 million	560,000 children below six years of age	To promote the healthy growth and holistic development of Eritrean children.
INDONESIA: *EARLY CHILDHOOD EDUCATION AND DEVELOPMENT PROJECT*	FY06–FY14	67.5 million (IDA credit)	127.7 million	738,000 children ages 0–6 years and their parents/caretakers in 3,000 poor communities	To improve poor children's overall development and readiness for further education, within a sustainable quality ECED system.
JAMAICA: *EARLY CHILDHOOD DEVELOPMENT PROJECT*	FY08–FY14	15 million (IBRD loan)	508.9 million	All children in Jamaica below six years old and their parents	To support the objectives of the National Strategic Plan to: (i) improve the monitoring of children's development, the screening of household-level risks, and the risk mitigation and early intervention systems; (ii) enhance the quality of early childhood schools and care facilities; and (iii) strengthen early childhood organizations and institutions.

table continues next page

Table 4.1 Summary of ECD Case Studies *(continued)*

Country and project	Duration	Bank contribution to ECD (in nominal US$)	Total project cost (in nominal US$)	Target population (end target, not necessarily number of beneficiaries reached)	Project development objective
JORDAN: *ECD COMPONENT OF EDUCATION REFORM FOR KNOWLEDGE ECONOMY*	FY03–FY16	Component cost: 6.2 million (five of IBRD funding)	370.0 million (total project)	Preschool-aged children, focusing particularly on disadvantaged groups (*exact number not available*)	To provide students enrolled in pretertiary education institutions in Jordan with increased levels of skills to participate in the knowledge economy. *ECD Component Objective:* Phase I: To enhance equity through public provision of KGII to low-income areas; Phase II: To expand access and enhance the quality of the ECD program in order to maximize children's learning potential
MEXICO: *ECD COMPONENT OF COMPENSATORY EDUCATION PROJECT*	FY10–FY14	Component Cost: 30 million (30 of IBRD loan)	166.7 million	58,685 children below six years old and their parents (52,670 parents; 1,761 pregnant women)	To improve access to ECD services and learning outcomes of children in the most marginalized municipalities of Mexico. *ECD Component Objective:* To improve the competencies and practices in caring for children and contribute to children's comprehensive development and school readiness
SENEGAL: *NUTRITION ENHANCEMENT PROGRAM (PHASES I AND II)*	FY02–FY13	29.7 million (2 phases of IDA credits)	62.6 million (Phase I: 20.2 million; Phase II: 42.4 million)	1.7 million children below 5 years old and pregnant and lactating women (Phase II)	To expand access to and enhance nutritional conditions of vulnerable populations, in particular those affecting growth of children under five in poor urban and rural areas

Source: World Bank data.

Note: ECD = early childhood development; ECED = early childhood education and development; FY = fiscal year; IBRD = International Bank for Reconstruction and Development; IDA = International Development Association.

development project, the Jordan early childhood development component of the education reform for knowledge economy project, the Mexico early childhood development component of the compensatory education project, and finally the Senegal nutrition enhancement project. Table 4.1 summarizes the seven operations detailed in this section, and appendix C provides additional details for each case study. In preparing brief case studies on the lessons learned from the projects, implementation completion reports (for closed operations), implementation supervision reports (for active operations), project appraisal documents, and other relevant research and articles related to the projects were reviewed. Additionally, TTLs and other World Bank staff involved in the specific operations were interviewed to gain a more in-depth and first-hand perspective on some of the successes as well as challenges of each of the seven operations. While this chapter presents key findings and lessons learned for each of the seven case studies, the following chapter presents a synthesis of the lessons learned across all seven projects and the broader ECD operations portfolio in order to suggest some the features that appear to be associated with successful ECD projects.

Bulgaria Social Inclusion Project (SIP)

In Bulgaria, children from poor households and ethnic minorities receive fewer years of schooling, which often leads to social exclusion later in life. This is also the case for preschools. While one year of preschool for six-year-olds is in principle compulsory, many children from poor families, rural areas, and minorities, in particular Roma, do not attend. In 2007, a $59 million loan was provided to the Government of Bulgaria (GoB) to promote social inclusion through a national school readiness program. The Social Inclusion Project (SIP) includes integrated social and childcare services with family-focused social services for children aged 0–3, and their parents, as well as formal kindergarten and childcare services for children aged 3–6. The project targets low-income and marginalized families, including children with disabilities and other special needs. Three main features and lessons from this project are worth emphasizing.

1. Municipalities were supported through finance and capacity building. Based on their needs, municipalities chose projects that they then managed locally from a menu of community subprojects, including both early childhood care and education (ECCE) services and infrastructure investments. To determine the eligibility of the municipalities as well as priority expenditures in each municipality, the project used targeting criteria, including the relative share of children and families on social assistance, municipal demand, efficiency requirements, and a sufficient number of potential beneficiaries and community stakeholders. In the design and early implementation phases, the project had success in working with and addressing the needs of local municipalities. Adapting to municipal demand was crucial. For example, when municipalities noted that conditionality clauses were unreasonable, the project was redesigned to better fit municipal demand. The project also promoted local capacity building for improved management and coordination. As of 2012, 133 municipal staff members had been trained in improved project management areas, including cross-sectoral cooperation, subcontracting and cooperation with nongovernmental organizations (NGOs), and accessing funding.

2. Parental involvement is emphasized. The SIP is designed to address the needs of both parents and children. Experience from previous piloted preschool programs in Bulgaria revealed that parental involvement in activities yielded higher outcomes for preschool-aged children. Therefore, the project is designed to promote cultural sensitivity and ensure that all parents would be included, particularly ethnic minorities. The SIP implementing agency will conduct intensive outreach in target communities, providing training to service providers on client-centered service delivery and supporting the development of relevant didactic material to benefit all children. The SIP will also rely on community-based organizations to tailor their services to the community needs.

3. The project intends to increase parental demand for services through fee reduction (conditional on participation in employment programs) and transportation to the centers. The project will compensate municipalities for reduced kindergarten fees so that it will be more affordable for low-income parents to send their children to kindergarten. Parents can access reduced kindergarten fees only if they also enroll in training and employment programs, which helped generate demand for those programs. In addition, transport will be offered to parents to increase the accessibility to ECCE services.

In November 2013, after facing delayed implementation due to budget spending limits, the project was extended by almost two years so that the integrated social inclusion services under the project could be implemented.

Eritrea Integrated Early Child Development (IECD) Project

As it recovered from political instability, Eritrea's public investments in early childhood services were very low in the 1990s. In 2000, a Bank loan supported the Government of Eritrea (GoE) through an Integrated Early Childhood Development (IECD) Project to increase access to and improve the quality of services in child health, child and maternal nutrition, early childhood care and education, and child protection for orphans. The project also focused on strengthening strategic communication and coordination mechanisms between government agencies to support the overall management of multisectoral ECD activities. Four main features and lessons from this project are worth emphasizing.

1. National ownership across ministries contributed to overall project success. Before the IECD operation even began, the GoE had recognized the importance of investing in young children and the stage was set for effective national facilitation of sector-specific ECD activities. National ministries and institutions had developed sector-specific ECD policies and programs, including the Ministry of Education's ECE policy framework, the Ministry of Health's policy guidelines on child and maternal health and nutrition, the Ministry of Agriculture's food security strategy, and the Ministry of Labor and Human Welfare's child protection programs for orphans. The IECD operation was designed to build upon the GoE's prior engagement in participating sectors and strengthen capacity at both the national and local levels. The strong national ownership also contributed to the project's sustainability: although Bank support was not extended after the original operation due to political factors unrelated to the operation itself, the GoE continued to support the delivery of integrated ECD services in the country.

2. *Clearly defined government roles across sectors and levels helped for coordinated implementation, but the project still faced challenges in monitoring and evaluation*. A Central Policy Committee, involving nine ministries, was formed to provide policy decisions and guidance on project activities. The Ministry of Education was identified as the lead ministry, and each ministry agreed upon its contribution to the project based on an operational manual which established clear institutional and implementation responsibilities at all administrative levels. In addition, each ministry agreed to specific financial procedures according to the multisectoral management and implementation of the project, which allowed for efficient flow of IECD funding. While the definition of roles ensured smooth implementation in general, the project still faced monitoring and evaluation challenges. Data from different ministries were uneven at different phases of the project, and it was difficult to monitor progress for all of the project's interventions in a streamlined manner. This improved as the project progressed, with increased attention to monitoring and evaluation capacity and management.

3. *Intersectoral committees at the national and regional levels were supported*. In coordination with the Central Policy Committee of Ministers, which served as the decision-making body for the project, a Project Management Team (PMT) coordinated national activities. Additionally, regional and subregional technical committees and working groups facilitated the project's activities at the regional and local levels. While the Ministry of Education served as the implementing agency for the project, the PMT, based in the Ministry of Local Government, coordinated project activities. The PMT served as a valuable link between sectors. It coordinated not only between the Ministry of Education and other line ministries but also between the central level and local coordinators. The IECD project supported significant capacity building for the PMT in financial management, procurement, communication, and leadership. The PMT made concerted efforts to promote the integrated package of delivery, including an integrated communication strategy and training manuals for multiple cross-sector training activities.

4. *Synergy between government and development partners was a success factor*. Compared to some other Sub-Saharan African ECD projects which did not achieve comparable positive results, the IECD project was based on existing partnerships in ECD services between the government and development agencies. Rather than starting completely new partnerships, the project built upon the GoE's prior engagement with partner agencies in implementation. For example, the implementation of the child health component achieved the target outcomes in part because of the close collaboration with United Nations Children's Fund (UNICEF), World Health Organization (WHO), and U.S. Agency for International Development (USAID) as these agencies already supported a number of maternal and child health programs, including a community-based Integrated Management of Childhood Illnesses and Growth Monitoring Promotion system.

Indonesia Early Childhood Education and Development (ECED) Project

In Indonesia, a variety of forms of early childcare and education (ECED) service provision exist, including formal kindergartens for 5–6-year-olds and a variety of nonformal, playgroups, childcare centers, and other early childhood units for children up to six years old. These services are more available in urban and wealthier areas of the country than in rural and poorer areas. With a variety of services and levels of coverage, discrepancies exist in the availability, quality, and regulatory measures for each service. In 2007, the Government of Indonesia (GoI) started with the support of the World Bank the ECED project to address this discrepancy in quality and coverage of services through a community-based approach. The ECED project supported policy development and system capacity building as well as community-based ECED service delivery. With the aim of increasing access to ECED services and enhancing school readiness, a package of interventions, including community facilitation, block grants to communities, and teacher training, was delivered to communities. Again, four main features and lessons from this project are worth emphasizing.

1. The project was designed using a community-driven development approach. Fifty districts were selected according to specific targeting criteria, including low participation rates in ECED services, low Human Development Index, high poverty rates, classification as a remote district, location in a border area, and a demonstrated commitment to developing an ECED agenda in their respective districts. The ECED project empowered community members to engage in participatory planning to improve local ECED services. Based on specific targeting criteria, districts awarded block grants to local communities. With the support of trained facilitators, communities were responsible for assessing existing resources and deciding which additional services (from a menu of ECED options) were needed in their communities.

2. The community grant model promoted district buy-in and financial sustainability. Starting at project inception, districts were responsible for allocating funds to ECD programs and upon completion of the project cycle the districts were to continue to support ECD services in the communities. While the project was designed to be sustainable, and presumably more so than other grant models, there were still risks in terms of sustainability. Indeed the midterm review of the project in 2011 identified as potential risk the fact that local governments and communities lacked the ability to sustain the community-based service delivery model. The Bank recommended an official handover of the project to the districts in order to ensure their support to service provision in villages where community grants had been fully disbursed. The Bank also requested that the National ECD Directorate guide districts in facilitating the collaboration of existing services with other village-based programs.

3. Mapping studies were used to identify coverage gaps. With the support of community facilitators, villages mapped existing ECED services and identified unmet needs to enhance the quality of existing services and establish new services as needed. Nearly 80 percent of the villages chose to establish new services. Villages could select services from a range of options, including playgroups, formal kindergartens, community health posts with ECED services, and outreach services, such as home-visiting or mother-child "play-and-learn" meetings. A midterm project evaluation revealed that the majority (90 percent) of the services offered in villages were center-based and satellite playgroups for children between the ages of three to six, with a majority of 3–4 age group. Outreach services (more suited for younger children) could not be fully implemented, since all the trained teachers were fully occupied with the 3- to 6-year-old children.

4. A built-in impact evaluation was highly valuable. The Bank is conducting a multiyear impact evaluation of the project to identify the effects of the interventions on enrollment and child development. At the time of design, 100 villages were randomly assigned to receive the package of interventions at the start of the project, and one year later, 100 control villages were to receive the package of interventions. Coordination challenges meant that the actual number of villages in each batch was slightly different (105 and 113 respectively.) Despite such deviations from design, initial rounds of data revealed that the ECED project had positive effects, including through increased enrollment rates and higher development outcomes for disadvantaged children. Additionally, evidence showed that communities with longer exposure to the project had higher enrollment rates. While data collected under the impact evaluation continue to provide policy-relevant information about the effectiveness of the project, it was challenging to implement in a rigorous way while also concurrently ensuring smooth operational processes and implementation.

Jamaica Early Child Development (ECD) Project

In 2008, the Government of Jamaica (GoJ) developed a results-focused National Strategic Plan (NSP) to advance ECD system performance. The NSP focuses on improving the quality and access to ECD services through strengthening sector organizations and institutions. In 2009, the World Bank provided a $15 million loan to Jamaica to cofinance the implementation of the NSP. Using a Sector-Wide Approach (SWAp), part of the loan supported the GoJ's plan to focus on ECD action areas including effective parenting education, preventive health care for 0–6-year-olds, screening and early intervention, safe and learner-centered ECE facilities, curriculum delivery, governance, and evidence-based decision making. With standard financing modalities, the loan also financed technical assistance to support the development of a national policy and screening, referral, and early intervention for at-risk children. As for the other projects, four interesting features and lessons from this project are emphasized below.

1. A single governing body promoted coordination across sectors. In 2003, the Early Childhood Commission (ECC) was legally established as the intersectoral agency to facilitate ECD planning across sectors and political parties. The ECC is institutionally based within the Ministry of Education, but it comprises representatives from across all key line ministries, as well as members from the political opposition. The ECC spearheaded the development of the NSP through a consensus-building process that validated and defined the national objectives for ECD. Responsibility for the country's ECD activities has now shifted from the Ministry of Education to the ECC, which serves as the single governing body to coordinate ECD activities within the NSP and is the implementing agency for the project.

2. Focusing on early intervention on the ground was an effective strategy. One of the NSP's key action areas was screening, diagnosis, and early intervention, particularly for at-risk children. Progress in this area has been largely attributed to the commitment and quality of efforts in the field. The GoJ has promoted these efforts through a variety of monitoring and coordination mechanisms across sectors. In the education sector, the mechanisms included a licensing system for early childhood practitioners, standards and accreditation system for early childhood parenting education programs, household-level screening and monitoring tools, and quality training on using tools to track at-risk households. As of September 2013, 61 development officers and 33 inspectors had been trained and worked in the field providing technical assistance and supporting ECD centers to reach minimum quality standards. Using a newly introduced national software system, the development officers could easily report ground-level indicators that were linked to NSP targets. In the health sector, recent legislation mandated that all children born after October 2010 receive Child Health Development Passports. This comprehensive document developed by the ECC, Ministry of Health, and Ministry of Education, tracks children from birth to age 17 years and contains each child's medical history, nutritional and oral health, childhood illnesses, injuries, referrals, parenting and safety tips, and school readiness assessment test records. As of June 2012, all clinics in Jamaica used the passport as a monitoring and risk screening device.

3. Disbursements linked to targets were an effective funding mechanism to leverage resources and ensure accountability. The project's results-based financing mechanism was structured such that funds were released every six months based upon the achievement of specific milestones connected to NSP actions. This disbursement-linked indicator (DLI) tool focused on achieving outputs and outcomes to improve services for children and parents. The ECC had a five-year fully-costed implementation plan for the NSP with more than 150 specific milestones. Loan disbursements were linked to 45 of these milestones. The ECC, in collaboration with sectoral ministries, evaluated whether targets were met. For each target achieved, the Bank disbursed $180,000 to the Ministry of Finance and Planning. This disbursement design incentivized the Ministry of Finance and Planning to provide necessary budgets, ensure the timely release of funds, and hold institutions accountable for achieving the targets. The Bank loan represented only 20 percent of the total cost of implementing the NSP, so that it helped the GoJ to implement activities sustainably, thereby promoting a robust ECD system beyond the project's life. The direct disbursements into the national budget through the Ministry of Finance and Planning promoted sustainability across sectors because each line ministry had its own budget for ECD targets tied to the NSP.

4. *The original project design was ambitious and had to be restructured in 2011.* While the project has been making progress, it initially faced obstacles in achieving its objectives due to a complex design and large number of indicators. The original results framework contained more than 70 indicators, many of them linked to disbursements. While the indicators were well aligned with the targets of the NSP, they had to be adjusted in order to align with the pace of the implementation of the NSP itself. The project was revised to reduce bottlenecks, address capacity constraints, and better facilitate monitoring of early childhood organizations in Jamaica.

Jordan ECD Component of Education Reform for the Knowledge Economy

In 2000, more than two-thirds of children in Jordan did not have access to preprimary education. Early childhood education (ECE) was not compulsory and few formal curriculum requirements were in place. With primarily private provision of ECE concentrated in urban and higher-income areas, poor households had unequal opportunities to access ECE. One component of the larger Education Reform for Knowledge Economy (ERfKE) operation was designed to promote readiness for learning through ECE services. The World Bank supported the Jordanian Ministry of Education in enhancing equity through public provision of kindergarten to low-income areas. This was achieved by expanding services for children at age five. The operation financed capacity building of a new preschool division in the Ministry of Education, professional development of early childhood educators, increased access to kindergarten for the poor, and community-based centers intended to improve parent and community participation. Upon achieving Phase I targets for kindergarten enrollment, professional development of kindergarten teachers, and enhanced ECE regulation and standards, the Bank's support for ECE was extended. Phase II of the ERfKE project included an ECE subcomponent directly linked with the government's new national strategy and plan of action for early childhood. Four interesting features and lessons from this project are emphasized below.

1. Supporting effective partnerships among stakeholders contributed to project success. Responsibilities for each institution were clearly defined during project preparation. The ECE component of the ERfKE project involved more than 15 organizations, including government departments, civil society organizations, and development partners. Consensus during the project's design phase set the stage for effective collaboration during implementation. Additionally, a Development Coordination Unit, comprised mostly of public officials located within the Ministry of Education, played the crucial role of coordination for the program.

2. Building institutional capacity in Ministry of Education to regulate ECE improved the quality of services delivered. In both phases of the ERfKE project, emphasis was placed on developing the ministry's capacity to enhance the quality of ECE throughout the country. The project supported the ministry in developing a digitized ECE curriculum and software and teaching guide, an ECE standards framework with indicators, a Quality Assurance Framework, as well as a Learning Readiness Assessment. To reach national-level achievements for improved quality and regulation of ECE, both the central- and local-level capacities were crucial. Supervisory committees at the central level guided the process, while field-level committees ensured ground-level implementation.

3. Involving parents and community members can lead to better outcomes for children. The Parent Involvement Program and the Better Parenting Program (cosponsored by UNICEF) initiatives had a positive impact on increasing household knowledge and understanding of the importance of early childhood care in the home and the community. In addition to enhancing parents' general awareness about their children's development, these programs engaged parents to play an active role in ensuring quality kindergarten classes. As a result of the program, parents have become more involved in volunteer activities in their children's kindergarten.

4. Teacher training was useful, but needed improvement. By the end of the ERfKE project's first phase, 93 percent of teachers had received in-service training on ECD. Training was provided to both the Ministry of Education and NGO-managed kindergarten teachers. Overall, the kindergarten teacher training was positively correlated to good teaching practices in the classroom. However, a study revealed that additional training for teachers did not result in a statistically significant effect on teaching practice in classrooms, suggesting that there might be too many training programs on similar themes. Instead of focusing on training the second phase of ERfKE was designed to strengthen ECE teacher professional development through the introduction of a performance assessment system for ECE professionals and paraprofessionals.

Mexico ECD Component of Compensatory Education Project

Established in the 1970s, the Mexican agency, Consejo Nacional para el Fomento Educativo (National Council for Education Development; CONAFE) has been serving hard-to-reach populations using innovative and low-cost service-delivery models. Recognizing the importance of helping children start off right, CONAFE launched in 1998 *Educación Inicial* to improve child development and school readiness for 0–4-year-olds and their parents. One of the largest programs in the Latin America and the Caribbean region, *Educación Inicial* reaches an estimated 400,000 children and their parents. The World Bank Compensatory Education Project (CEP) ($100 million) aimed to increase the breadth of the program to include 172 of the poorest and hardest to reach municipalities in the country. CEP included an ECD component ($30 million) that was designed to strengthen the *Educación Inicial* program. CONAFE's approach uses existing assets, such as preschools and public spaces, for meeting areas and a network of volunteers to teach the parenting education classes. This community-based approach has been successful and cost effective in improving parenting practices and contributes to children's comprehensive development and school readiness. The measures help ensure that high-quality services were provided to CONAFE's target population, while keeping costs to a reasonable $112 per child per year, thereby allowing the government to serve large numbers of beneficiaries in a sustainable manner. Three interesting features and lessons from this project are emphasized below.

1. Including fathers as beneficiaries for parenting education is important, albeit very difficult. Special sessions aimed at fathers were designed to address the issue of fathers' underrepresentation in parenting education programs, and promote their participation in childrearing. By targeting fathers explicitly, CONAFE hoped to signal to them the importance of being involved in their children's development. Recognizing that fathers have different needs and levels of knowledge from mothers with regard to childrearing and may be unavailable to attend sessions at the usual time, CONAFE offered five sessions tailored to them. In addition, offering sessions only for fathers created a safe space for them to share and learn among their peers. Success in getting father's to attend has been mixed, however: incentivizing the participation of fathers proved much harder than expected, though some success was found when the program was administered in partnership with the municipal government.

2. Early stimulation interventions were emphasized. An evaluation conducted in 2009 revealed that while CONAFE's approach was demonstrating good results, the model was not fully exploiting the opportunity for providing direct early stimulation services. The latest generation of *Educación Inicial* trained volunteers interacting directly with the children during the sessions, to both maximize the presence of the volunteer and provide more hands-on training to parents. Special early stimulation sessions for children below four were also incorporated, in an effort to maximize impact.

3. ECD programs were adapted to better serve indigenous groups. In order to maximize the potential benefits of the *Educación Inicial* for indigenous communities in Mexico's most marginalized municipalities, the Bank, through the project's Indigenous Peoples Plan (IPP), provided technical assistance for the adaptation of educational materials. This involved adapting existing CONAFE materials for the specific needs of indigenous children and their parents. Among the different elements considered for adaptation were the photos, graphics, language, and format. Recommendations were developed following a series of consultations with indigenous leaders and members of the communities, and testing of proposed revisions (however, it is yet to be determined the extent to which these actions will have an impact on better reaching indigenous groups).

Senegal Nutrition Enhancement Program (Phases I and II)

In 2002, the Government of Senegal launched the Nutrition Enhancement Program (NEP) to provide multisectoral support for nutrition and enhance nutritional conditions for children below five and pregnant and lactating women. It included a community-based Growth Monitoring and Promotion component and an Integrated Management of Childhood Illnesses system with maternal counseling, home visits, and cooking demonstrations. Upon reducing the prevalence of underweight children in the three targeted regions in Phase I, the project was extended for a second phase to expand coverage in all 14 regions of the country. As of 2012, the government had expanded the community nutrition program to reach more than 60 percent of the target population.

1. Identifying a national nutrition focal point was an effective implementation strategy. In preparing the project, the government and the World Bank recognized the need for a multisectoral coordination commission to lead implementation across health, nutrition, agriculture, water, and sanitation sectors. The Cellule de Lutte contre la Malnutrition (Coordination unit for the reduction of malnutrition; CLM) was established under the supervision of the prime minister's office as an independent government agency responsible for implementing the national nutrition policy. The CLM was not institutionally based within any of the line ministries and it has proven to be highly receptive to institutional strengthening and team building outside of the bureaucracy that can affect other agencies. The CLM developed good implementation ability and trust from the ground to the central level. It directed responsibility to the lowest level possible, which reduced inefficient management at the central level, as well as provided opportunities for adaptation at the local level.

2. Building inclusive partnerships at the local level helped. Throughout the project, strong emphasis was placed on both results and "learning by doing." This allowed implementing partners at the local level to develop their own strategies, while still receiving constant support from the central level. Local partners were responsible and accountable for much of the operation on the ground. This included developing training manuals and materials, selecting nutrition aides, and overseeing project activities and results. An effective system of monitoring and evaluation was also developed at the local level. Routine monitoring of data from the community level occurred on a monthly basis. The monitoring system was intentionally designed to be simple and easily adaptable to existing monitoring systems.

3. *The sectorwide approach for nutrition proved advantageous.* While the CLM operated as an independent institution, it collaborated with sector ministries to seek synergies with other major national programs for children. For example, the health and nutrition sectors came together to integrate the promotion of feeding practices with the standard delivery of essential health services. The project integrated Growth Monitoring and Promotion with the Ministry of Health's existing community-based Integrated Management of Childhood Illnesses system. Due to this synergetic effect between the two institutions, the NEP project became a mechanism for delivering other essential health and nutrition services provided by existing programs. Throughout the project life, a variety of interventions, such as distribution of insecticide-treated bed nets and vitamin A supplementation were progressively added to NEP. In addition to health and nutrition services, other programs such as social cash transfers and food production/transformation support for households with children under five have also been incorporated into the NEP under the sectorwide approach.

4. *Community mobilization helped change behavior.* During monthly Growth Monitoring and Promotion visits, trained community members counseled caregivers on making decisions regarding feeding practices and child care. The counseling was based on the child's monthly weighing results and was designed to be a negotiation process in which nutrition aids worked with caregivers to gradually improve their behavior. This community-based behavior change communication strategy[1] proved to be effective in changing behavior and reducing malnutrition, without the use of external food assistance. Another innovative aspect of the project's community mobilization activity was the development of grandmother clubs. Embracing the tradition in which older women assist younger women in health care, older women were brought together to discuss family and child health issues. With the intention of promoting solidarity in practicing healthy childrearing, rather than receiving educational sessions, grandmothers in the clubs were simply provided a space to discuss factors that affect their daughters or daughters-in-law (who generally live in their homes).

Note

1. Global Strategy for Infant and Young Child Feeding Promotion (WHO and UNICEF 2003).

CHAPTER 5

Lessons Learned from Operations

Abstract

While the success of every project is certainly based on the context, many early childhood development (ECD) projects have noteworthy features in common. This chapter identifies common opportunities, as well as challenges, related to designing, implementing, and achieving results in ECD projects. It reviews issues related to ECD project design as well as effective features that have contributed to the success of many ECD projects. Lessons are largely drawn from the seven cases described in the report. However, Implementation Completion Results (ICRs)[1] and program documentation from other closed ECD operations also informed the lessons in this section.

Considerations for Effective ECD Project Design

Understand existing institutional arrangements and coordinating mechanisms. Given the complex nature of ECD projects, which are often multisectoral, designing targeted activities and components can be a challenge. As ECD projects tend to be decentralized, it can be difficult to link a national ECD agenda to local service delivery. A common obstacle in many ECD projects is balancing the depth and breadth of desired interventions. It is important to understand the country context to determine the feasibility of working with multiple ministries and agencies, which may determine the scope of domains covered. Additionally, it is useful to consider whether mechanisms are in place (or if it is viable to create new ones) that will ensure a central government's coordination with the level of service delivery.

Use simple, reliable, and easily measurable indicators to assess the achievement of a project development objective (PDO) and the intermediate outcomes. Projects are unsatisfactory in reaching desired outcomes when indicators are not aligned with actual project activities. For example, one project listed an indicator for the number of children below age seven with vaccinations, but the particular project did not deliver immunizations. Conversely, in other projects, some indicators that are directly related to project activities, such as improved child development, may be excluded from results frameworks. In these cases, the intervention's success is not adequately measured. Every category within a component (for example: capacity building of early childhood care and education [ECCE] service providers) should have a reliable and direct indicator (number of kindergarten teachers, municipal staff, health workers, and so on trained).

Select indicators that are within the scope of the project and its implementation period rather than pegging them to the higher level outcomes. It can be difficult to select appropriate indicators because some indicators or outcomes related to nutrition or school readiness may be achieved only in the long term. For example, when some projects monitored malnutrition, there were often complexities related to measuring a specific project's impact on the reduction of malnutrition. In many cases, the reduction of malnutrition is a higher-level outcome that might be more appropriate for a country strategy than for a specific ECD intervention. When a project cannot necessarily account for external factors related to food security and nutritional status, the use of malnutrition prevalence as an outcome indicator will not necessarily measure the performance of a project. In these cases, outcome indicators focused on changes in conditions (such as increased overall program coverage, increase in percentage of infants exclusively breastfed, and so on) may be more appropriate.

ECD is often highlighted for its link to "school readiness," and thus, tracking primary school performance (such as primary school repetition and dropout rates) may seem like a reasonable indicator of program impact. However, project periods often may be too short to find an impact from integrated ECD activities on children during primary school. Improvements in cognitive development may take longer to manifest than a given project period allows to monitor. Outcomes resulting in improved cognitive development, such as primary school performance, might be influenced by an intervention, but in the longer term. In this case, appropriate child development assessments during preschool or at school entry or output indicators such as preprimary enrollment and attendance or on time school enrollment may be more suitable measures. Table 5.1 presents examples of PDO indicators, taken from the selected case studies. In addition to PDO indicators, intermediate outcome indicators, or results indicators, are also valuable tools in monitoring the success of projects.

Carefully design the Monitoring and Evaluation (M&E) framework, as it is an essential element in a successful ECD project. Given that ECD projects require links both across sectors and across levels of government links, a complex M&E framework is necessary. During project design, the capacity of participating line ministries in both managing and coordinating data collection must be addressed. Projects can fall short when there is inadequate M&E capacity and/or roles for monitoring progress are not clearly defined. Multiple organizations, including the World Bank, Ministries of Education or Health, implementing agencies, and/or service providers may be involved in the M&E process. The availability and consistency of data from this array of different stakeholder groups can be challenging to coordinate. Bank staff in projects such

Table 5.1 Examples of PDO Indicators

Theme	PDO indicators
ECCE	• EDI scores (*Early Development Instrument*) for children entering kindergarten/1st grade (EDI locally adapted) • Gross enrollment rate in kindergarten • Number of children 0–4 years who attend at least 80 percent of the ECD sessions • Repetition and dropout rates from primary grade 1 to grade 2
Child nutrition	• Percentage of children under 12 months who have received the complete growth and development scheme • Percentage of children under 36 months who have received complete growth and development scheme according to their age in the areas of intervention • Nutritional program coverage of children under the age of five in rural areas • Proportion of children exclusively breastfed until six months • Percentage of underweight children under six years of age in project areas
Child and maternal health	• Proportion of pregnant women and children under five sleeping under bed nets • Number of children screened for risks using child health passport • Health centers offering well-child clinics that are accredited
Child protection	• Successful reunification of orphans with nearest relatives • Number of children with disabilities and other special needs enrolled in mainstream kindergarten/preschool • Beneficiary households with children 0–6 years old screened for child development risks

Source: World Bank data.
Note: ECCE = early childhood care and education; ECD = early childhood development; PDO = project development objective.

as those in Senegal and Jordan learned that ensuring various data sources and supportive feedback and clarifying roles for internal and external M&E was essential.

Despite a multilevel, multisector implementation process, a single framework that consistently evaluates progress has been found to be an effective strategy for streamlining M&E. For example, because the Senegal Nutrition Enhancement Program (NEP) project had explicit arrangements for agency coordination for a single M&E framework and process, costs were reduced and the duplication of efforts was avoided.

National Commitment

Consider existing political commitment to ECD at the national level. Given that ECD may not traditionally have an institutional home in many countries, it is crucial for national leadership to recognize the importance of ECD. It is important to note, however, that this is just one essential ingredient to ensure effective

ECD operation implementation. Strong commitment at the highest level (typically in the Ministry of Education [MoE]) must be complemented by necessary capacity of technical-level teams.

Recognize the necessity of a national ECD champion. Lessons from ECD projects reveal that driving forces for ECD reforms must come from within partner governments, rather than imposed by external agencies. This was seen in Jordan, where the early childhood education (ECE) component aligned with the government's newly established ECE strategy. The Queen of Jordan, Rania Al Abdullah, contributed to the success of the Bank's ECD activities. Serving as a national champion for ECD efforts in Jordan, Queen Rania publically advocated about the importance of ECD. In Eritrea, the Integrated Early Childhood Development (IECD) operation built on the government's prior engagement in participating sectors. In Jamaica, the government's commitment has been an essential element of the progress of the ECD project. Through the already established National Strategic Plan (NSP), the national ministries demonstrated their commitment to sector-specific ECD activities, before the project even began. The Jamaica case also demonstrates that government commitment is not only necessary at the central level, but is equally, if not more, essential at the ground level. Government staff commitment to the level of service provision is necessary across area, from management of information systems to ensuring effective ECD practitioner training and monitoring quality compliance. The national government now finances the salaries of development officers and ECD inspectors who work in the field. The inclusion of these field staff to the national government's payroll not only is an indicator of the commitment of the national government, but it also ensures the sustainability of these essential activities after project completion.

Local Ownership

Encourage local government participation, starting at the beginning of a project. Communities need sufficient time to understand the benefits of interventions. In interventions such as the Eritrean IECD, the Mexican Compensatory Education Project (CEP), and the Indonesian Early Childhood Education and Development (ECED), communities needed adequate support to develop their own plans for sustainable implementation. Sustainability of projects is threatened when local districts are not aware of the benefits of ECD interventions or their roles in supporting them. In the Mexican CEP operation, a municipal-based management pilot was designed to strengthen the role of local authorities in mobilizing communities to value early childhood. In the Indonesian ECED project, facilitators focused on building capacity in each district and raising awareness about the importance of ECD. At the community level, key stakeholders had an active role in improving the quality of services. This community-driven development approach is cited as playing a key role in the success of the project.

Design ECD projects to promote local ownership. Ensuring local ownership can often be challenging; often, a certain level of local ownership must be in place already for this approach to be successful. While it is clear that local ownership is important, it can be difficult to actually incorporate into project. In Indonesia, this issue was addressed by including demonstrated commitment from local governments as a criterion for project participation. Qualification for participation was contingent on whether local governments had in place an ECD action plan, existing ECD unit and staff equipped to manage and coordinate with stakeholders, and an ECD budget allocation. Experience from Indonesia shows that local government capacity and commitment is essential, even if this means that some of the neediest districts are ultimately excluded from a community-driven project.

Include parents to promote local ownership of ECD services. Evidence from Bank operations suggests that empowering parents through support and increased knowledge can both preserve and improve on gains from traditional ECD services. Additionally, parental education can be a strategy for increasing demand for improved quality services and providers in ECCE. When parents are informed, they are more likely to hold service providers accountable for quality provision of services to their children. Parental education programs, such as the Consejo Nacional Fomento Educación (National Council for Education Development; CONAFE) program in Mexico and the Better Parenting Program in Jordan, teach parents and caregivers about the domains of child development and positive parenting in the home. In Jamaica, not only are parental education activities promoted, but the project went one step further by also addressing the issue of quality. The Early Childhood Commission (ECC) (Jamaica's ECD focal point) has created an accreditation system for ECD parenting education programs as well as established a parenting commission responsible for enforcing quality ECD services.

Coordination across Sectors and Levels

Recognize that the number of sectors to engage in a given Bank ECD operation is very country specific and a contextualized approach is best. Before discussing multisector projects, it is important to note that many single-sector projects, which make up roughly two-thirds of the ECD portfolio of operations, can still effectively address a targeted domain of child development. While evidence suggests that children's development occurs across different domains and requires interventions in multiple sectors (Neuman and Devercelli 2013), the best strategy to achieve coordination across sectors is country specific. Multisector or single-sector projects can both achieve positive effects in a country's ECD system. However, mechanisms to promote a certain level of coordination of sectors and institutions are recommended (World Bank 2012). As described below, the best approaches vary by country.

Start the collaborative process at the project design phase to ensure effective partnership arrangements during implementation. Many ECD projects require a great deal of coordination by national line ministries, partner agencies, regional governments, and local governments. A handful of projects included institutional strengthening at national, district, and local levels. For example, in Eritrea, training was provided to line managers and technical experts in various sectors to facilitate achieving common inputs. In Jordan, the MoE worked with more than 10 stakeholder agencies at both the central and ground levels to develop a national ECE strategy. In Bulgaria, the central government facilitated training of municipal staff for improved project management and cross-sectoral coordination.

Establish an ECD anchor to encourage smooth implementation of Bank operations, as well as existing and future ECD policies and programs. The institutional arrangements for ECD focal points vary by country context. In many cases, an ECD anchor is based within a ministry (often the MoE). In Indonesia, for example, the ECED Directorate was established under the Ministry of National Education. Similarly, the ECC, institutionally based within the Jamaican MoE, has served as the single governing body to coordinate activities across line ministries.

In other cases, ECD project implementation has been more effective when ECD focal points are located outside a particular ministerial structure. The success of the Cellule de Lutte contre la Malnutrition (Coordination unit for the reduction of malnutrition; CLM), which is the national nutrition focal point for the NEP operation in Senegal, has been specifically attributed to the fact that the agency is not tied to any line ministries. Given its placement outside the ministries, the CLM did not face sectoral limitations and was able to function with fewer burdens associated with bureaucracy.

Targeting Disadvantaged Children

Design interventions to identify and target the most vulnerable or marginalized children. Embracing a great potential for impact, many World Bank ECD projects target the most disadvantaged children in a country's population. In Bulgaria, the SIP operation is targeted to low-income and marginalized families. In Indonesia, participating districts were selected on the basis of a number of criteria, including low Human Development Index and high poverty rates. The ECD project in Jordan focuses particularly on preschool-aged children from disadvantaged groups. And, Mexico's CONAFE program is designed to serve poor rural and indigenous communities. While evidence clearly shows that children coming from the lowest socioeconomic status are the most likely to benefit from ECCE interventions (Naudeau et al. 2011), the challenge is often in reaching those children. Some projects are designed to expand coverage in areas with previously poor access to ECCE. Other projects, such as in Mexico, Bulgaria, and Indonesia, use specific targeting mechanisms to select municipalities and/or communities based on poverty rates.

Sociocultural Relevance

Take into account the unique set of needs and priorities for children within a particular community. A challenge for Bank staff and partners is the adequate adaptation of ECD interventions to the diverse local languages, beliefs, and practices. The issue of sociocultural relevance must be considered at all levels. At the central level, policies and program materials can be translated into native languages, as was done in Eritrea. The Government of Eritrea translated its new national ECD policies into the eight official local languages, which helped gain support for policy implementation at the district and community levels.

At the local level, the CEP operation in Mexico offers a good example of an ECD project designed to cater to the culture and environment of rural and indigenous communities. First, the implementing agency, CONAFE, has experience working with indigenous people in rural Mexico and is able to make the national program relevant and accessible to the local communities. Second, local promoters receive training to raise awareness about the local culture and beliefs and learn how to transmit messages that are culturally sensitive to the local concept of childcare and family dynamics. Training materials also are tailored to local language and cultural factors.

Address particular caregiving traditions within local cultures. In Senegal, older women in the community are the authority on tradition, health care, and childrearing. The NEP project in Senegal recognizes the powerful role that mother-in-laws and other senior women play in childrearing and children's health. Establishing grandmother clubs has proven an effective strategy that aligns with Senegalese caregiving traditions to promote healthy growth and development of young children. Similarly, in Mexico, the CONAFE program caters to fathers, who traditionally play less of a caregiving role. Sessions offered only to fathers take into account the different needs and levels of knowledge from mothers.

Knowledge Exchange

Build upon best practices of ECD policy and programs from other countries. Technical expertise has been strengthened in World Bank ECD operations through drawing lessons from other countries. For example, in Eritrea, along with other African operations in ECD, members of the technical support committee strengthened their leadership and management capacity through participation in the Early Childhood Development Virtual University (ECDVU) program. ECDVU is a capacity building program piloted in 10 Sub-Saharan African countries that provides a three-year, web-based Master's degree or diploma in ECD capacity, leadership, and network enhancement. The accredited program, institutionally based at the University of Victoria, creates a network of committed learners to learn from international ECD experts as well as share from fellow students also working at middle management levels in national ECD systems. Upon participating in ECDVU, members of the Government of Eritrea's technical ECD team contributed to the curriculum design and implementation of the Eritrea IECD operation.

Another exchange of knowledge was sparked between the continued success of Mexico's innovative parenting support program and the consistent accomplishments of Jamaica's National Strategic Plan. Representatives involved in the operations in the two countries saw an opportunity to learn from each other and delegations from Mexico and Jamaica engaged in an exchange of strategies through a series of videoconferences and field visits. Through this process, Mexican representatives were driven to start the development of their own national ECD strategy as well as create an interagency team to work on common interests. And, representatives from Jamaica took what they learned from Mexico to highlight community ownership of parenting programs within its National Parenting Support Policy.

Note

1. Of the 89 operations, 26 had ICRs available. Of those 26, only 2 were self-standing ECD projects, 6 were projects with ECD components, and 18 were projects with ECD subcomponents. It is important to note, particularly for projects with ECD subcomponents that the ratings should not be misinterpreted as ratings for ECD. In many cases, these subcomponents were a very small proportion of the overall project and were only briefly touched upon in the ICRs (if at all).

CHAPTER 6

Trends in Analytical, Advisory, and Partnership Work

Abstract

On purpose, this study was primarily devoted to an analysis of trends in World Bank operational commitments for early childhood development (ECD) as well as the lessons learned from operations. But the importance of the Bank's analytical and advisory activities should not be underestimated. This chapter reviews trends in the Bank's economic and sector work (ESW) and technical assistance (TA) work related to ECD for the period FY 2001 to FY 2013. A total of 107 activities focused on ECD or with important ECD components were identified with total funding of $55.4 million (in US$ of 2013). The number of analytical and advisory activities increased especially in the last few years, as observed for operations. As a share of the human development (HD) portfolio, funding for analytical work on ECD decreased over time, but as a share of the number of activities, the emphasis placed on ECD increased. The regions with the largest number of activities were Latin America and Africa and the education sector led the way.

Investments in Analytical, Advisory, and Partnership Work

Between FY 2001 and FY 2013, the World Bank invested $51 million (in real terms) through 107 analytical, advisory, and partnership activities. These activities include economic and sector work (ESW), technical assistance (TA), impact evaluations (IE), programmatic approaches (PA), knowledge products (KP), and Global Partnerships and Program (GPP). As was done for operations, for the activities led by the education, health, nutrition, and population sector (HNP), and social protection sectors, using the methodology described in chapter 2, a total of 107 analytical and advisory activities focused on ECD were identified for the period from FY 2001 to FY 2013. Total funding for the period amounted to $55.4 million in real terms (US$ of 2013).[1] Table 6.1 displays the number of activities and funding for each task.

Table 6.2 and figures 6.1 and 6.2 display the number of activities and the corresponding financial commitments to fund those activities by fiscal year of approval. The 54 activities implemented over the period represent an average of 8.2 activities per year, with an average of $4.26 million per year in funding

Table 6.1 Analytical, Advisory, and Partnership Activities, by Type (FY 2001 to FY 2013)

Type of activity	Number of tasks	Funding for AAA tasks (US$ million)	Funding for AAA in 2013 US$ (US$ million)
Economic and sector work (ESW)	32	6.59	7.13
Global Partnerships and Programs (GPP)	8	11.88	13.70
Technical assistance (TA)	44	17.99	19.54
Impact evaluations (IE)	16	13.11	13.17
Programmatic approaches (PA)	3	1.04	1.04
Knowledge products (KP)	4	0.85	0.85
Total	107	51.45	55.43

Source: World Bank data.
Note: AAA = analytical advisory activities; FY = fiscal year.

Table 6.2 Trend in the Number of and Funding for ECD-Related Analytical and Partnership Activities by Year

FY	Number of tasks	Funding for tasks (US$ million)	Adjustment factor from US GDP deflator[a]	Funding for in 2013 US$ (US$ million)
FY01	2	1.27	82.9	1.62
FY02	5	1.04	84.4	1.31
FY03	2	0.10	85.9	0.13
FY04	3	8.06	87.8	9.72
FY05	5	1.41	90.5	1.65
FY06	5	1.41	93.5	1.60
FY07	3	0.27	96.2	0.29
FY08	10	8.25	98.2	8.89
FY09	9	3.82	99.9	4.05
FY10	11	4.16	100.4	4.38
FY11	13	2.04	102.2	2.11
FY12	8	4.28	104.1	4.35
FY13	31	15.33	105.8	15.33
Total	107	51.45	n.a.	55.43
Average per year	8.23	3.96	n.a.	4.26

Source: World Bank data.
Note: ECD = early childhood development; FY = fiscal year; GDP = gross domestic product; n.a. = not applicable.
a. Adjustment based on average of quarterly U.S. GDP Implicit Price Deflator for each fiscal year (U.S. Department of Commerce, Bureau of Economic Analysis).

Trends in Analytical, Advisory, and Partnership Work

Figure 6.1 HD ECD Analytical, Advisory, and Partnership Activities, US$ million (US$ of 2013)

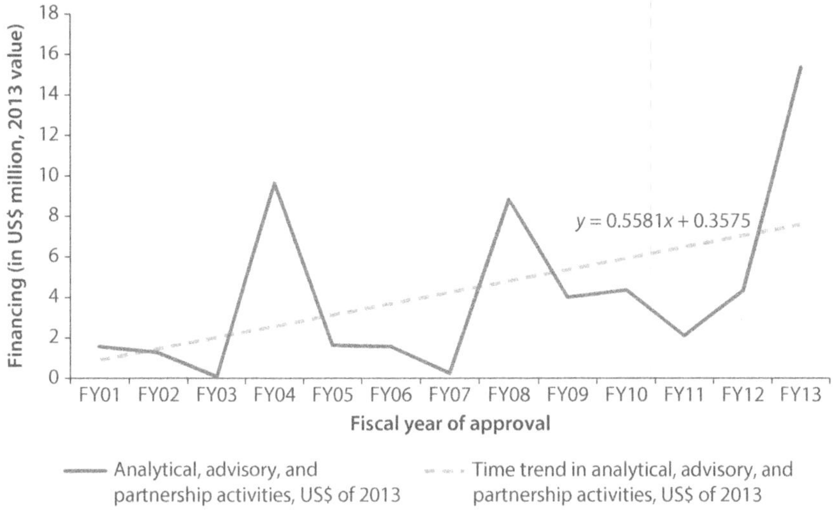

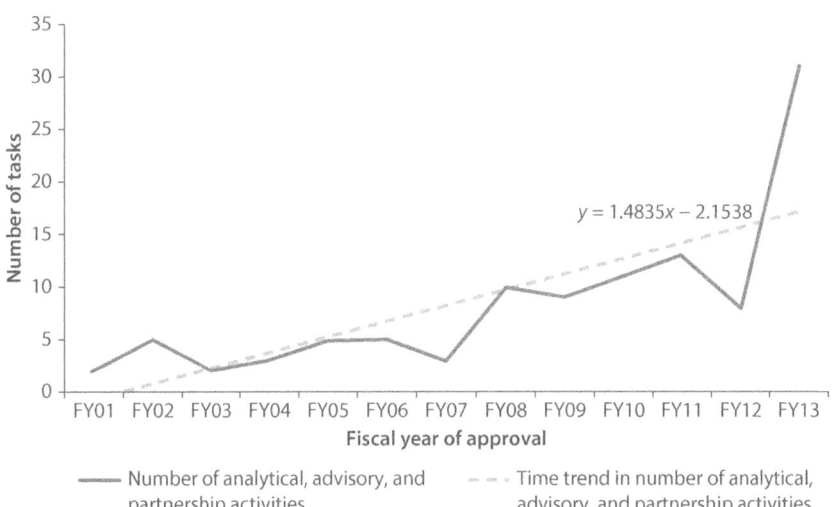

Source: World Bank data.
Note: ECD = early childhood development; HD = human development.

Figure 6.2 Trend in Number of HD ECD Analytical, Advisory, and Partnership Activities

Source: World Bank data.
Note: ECD = early childhood development; HD = human development.

(US$ of 2013). As displayed in figures 6.1 and 6.2, both the number of tasks and funding dramatically increased in FY 2013. While the average number of analytical advisory activities (AAA) activities between FY 2001 and FY 2012 was six per tasks at $3.4 million, in 2013 alone, there were 31 activities totalling US$15.3 million.

Analytical, Advisory, and Partnership Activities by Sector and Region

Across sectors, the education sector supported the most analytical, advisory, and partnership work. Table 6.3 provides data on funding and the number of analytical, advisory, and partnership activities by region and by sector. The largest number of activities and the bulk of the funding were allocated by the education sector, followed by the HNP sector and then social protection. This may reflect a higher interest in ESW and TA work for preschools and early learning, but it probably also reflects in part the fact that institutionally, the ECD work is located in the education department at the World Bank, with most of the regional focal points for ECD being education specialist.

In terms of geographic allocations, the region that benefitted from the largest amount of funding for ESW and TA was Africa, followed by Latin America. These were also the two regions that benefited from the largest ECD commitments in the International Bank for Reconstruction and Development/International Development Association (IBRD/IDA) portfolio, but the order of the two regions in the ranking is reversed for AAA and partnerships. This may reflect the fact that with a larger number of countries in the Africa region, there are more opportunities to conduct analytical, advisory, and partnership work in that region than in the other regions Map 6.2 provides a map to visualize the

Table 6.3 Analytical, Advisory, and Partnership Activities: Number of Tasks and Funding (in US$ of 2013) by Region and Sector

	Education		Health, nutrition and population		Social protection		All three sectors	
	Number of projects	Funding (US$ millions)	Number of projects	Funding (US$ millions)	Number of projects	Funding (US$ millions)	Number of projects	Funding (US$ millions)
Africa	18	11.39	9	6.35	2	2.11	29	19.85
East Asia and the Pacific	7	1.68	5	3.69	0	0.00	12	5.36
Europe and Central Asia	8	2.09	1	0.40	0	0.00	9	2.49
Latin America and the Caribbean	10	2.67	4	1.42	2	0.29	16	4.37
Middle East and North Africa	9	2.31	2	0.56	0	0.00	11	2.87
South Asia	3	0.55	8	4.05	0	0.00	11	4.60
World	13	12.39	6	3.51	0	0.00	19	15.90
Total	68	33.08	35	19.96	4	2.40	107	55.43

Source: World Bank data.

Map 6.1 Distribution of HD ECD Analytical, Advisory, and Partnership Activities

Source: World Bank data.

countries that benefited from analytical, advisory, and partnership work with a coloring scheme based on the number of activities implemented in each beneficiary country. In addition to the country-specific tasks, there were 18 global tasks, eight Africa regional tasks, six Middle East and North Africa regional tasks, three Latin America and the Caribbean regional tasks, and one task each in both Europe and Central Asia and South Asia.

ECD Share in HD Analytical and Partnership Activities

As a share of total analytical and partnership activities in the HD portfolio as a whole, ECD activities appear to have increased over time (see table 6.4). This upward trend exists for both the share of activities (as displayed in figure 6.3) and the share of funding for activities (as displayed in figure 6.4).

Similar to the operational portfolio, it is clear that in recent years the three HD practices have advanced their priority in ECD through analytical and partnership activities. In 2001, only 2 percent of these activities were focused on ECD, whereas in 2013, more than one in 10 HD analytical and partnership activities were focused on ECD. Furthermore, 42.8 percent of funding for these activities was allocated to ECD activities in 2013, a much higher proportion than in earlier years.

As displayed in table 6.4, over the period as a whole, ECD represented 3.9 percent of the number of HD analytical and partnership activities and 11.8 percent of funding for these activities.

Investing in Early Childhood Development • http://dx.doi.org/10.1596/978-1-4648-0403-8

Table 6.4 Share of ECD in HD Analytical and Partnership Portfolio by Year

	ECD			HD			ECD as share of HD portfolio	
FY	Number of activities	Total funding for activities ($M, 2013)	Average funding per activity ($M)	Number of activities	Total funding for activities ($M, 2013)	Average amount	ECD share of activities (%)	ECD share of funding (%)
FY01	2	1.6	0.8	97	19.4	0.2	2.1	8.4
FY02	5	1.3	0.3	124	19.3	0.2	4.0	6.8
FY03	2	0.1	0.1	158	12.8	0.1	1.3	1.0
FY04	3	9.7	3.2	214	41.2	0.2	1.4	23.6
FY05	5	1.6	0.3	215	37.8	0.2	2.3	4.4
FY06	5	1.6	0.3	179	28.3	0.2	2.8	5.6
FY07	3	0.3	0.1	212	32.7	0.2	1.4	0.9
FY08	10	8.9	0.9	205	46.5	0.2	4.9	19.1
FY09	9	4.1	0.5	210	27.1	0.1	4.3	14.9
FY10	11	4.4	0.4	228	39.0	0.2	4.8	11.2
FY11	13	2.1	0.2	211	42.1	0.2	6.2	5.0
FY12	8	4.4	0.5	209	44.2	0.2	3.8	9.8
FY13	31	15.3	0.5	258	35.8	0.1	12.0	42.8
Total	107	55.4	n.a.	2,520	426.3	n.a.	4.2	n.a.
Average per year	8.2	4.3	0.2	193.8	32.8	0.2	3.9	11.8

Source: World Bank data.
Note: ECD = early childhood development; FY = fiscal year; HD = human development; n.a. = not applicable.

Figure 6.3 Share of Projects with ECD Components in HD Analytical/Partnership Portfolio

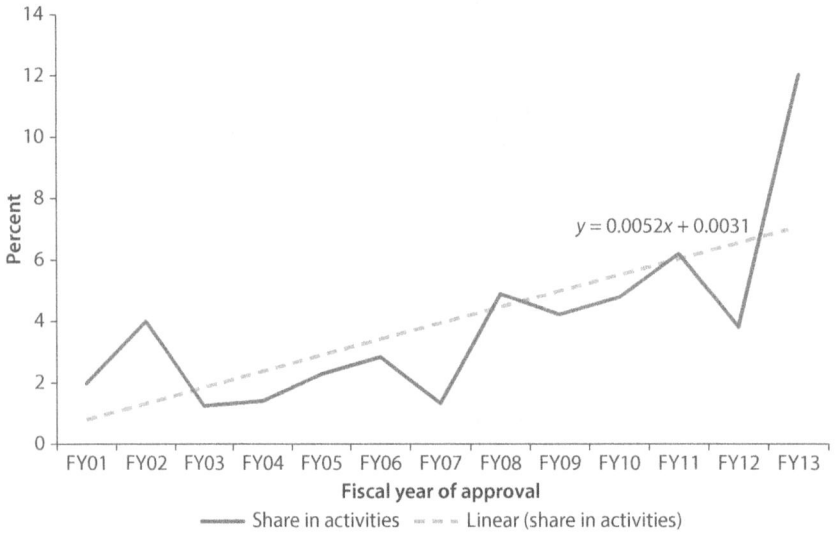

Source: World Bank data.
Note: ECD = early childhood development; HD = human development.

Figure 6.4 Share of Funding for Activities with ECD Components in HD Analytical/Partnership Portfolio

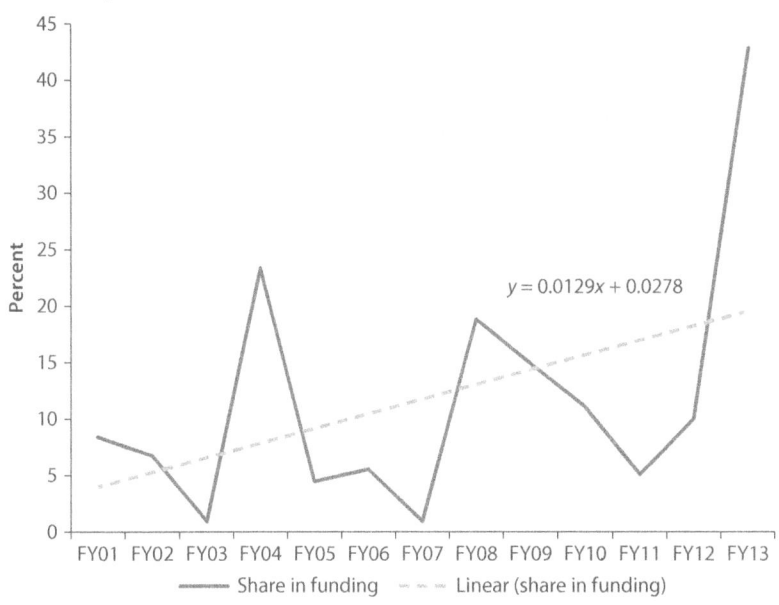

Source: World Bank data.
Note: ECD = early childhood development; HD = human development.

Examples of Analytical, Advisory, and Partnership Work

The analytical, advisory, and partnership activities reviewed in this chapter represent a wide range of focus. These activities offer promising examples of new knowledge and partnerships focused on ECD and often serve as a catalyst for increased operational investments. In addition to the examples presented here, the next chapter takes a more comprehensive look at several recent initiatives of ECD approaches that represent promising strategies as the World Bank looks at its next phase of ECD investments.

In 2010, *The Promise of Early Childhood Development in Latin America and the Caribbean* was published, which stemmed from an ESW activity implemented in FY 2008. The book reviews a selection of early childhood education, health, and nutrition programs in the Latin American and the Caribbean region. It presents evidence-based arguments for increased ECD investments in the region and emphasizes the need for more rigorous evaluations of ECD programming. This work also discusses the policy implications for scaling up ECD investments through multisectoral government policies.

The Middle East and North Africa regional Early Childhood Development studies, stemming from FY 2011 ESW, investigated the status of ECD in the Middle East and North Africa region. Bank colleagues conducted an analysis of health, nutrition, child care, and early education indicators, mapped local and national institutional capacity in ECD, and took inventory of major ECD

Table 6.5 Ongoing SIEF-Funded ECD Impact Evaluations at the World Bank: First Round (2012): Early Childhood Nutrition, Health, and Development Cluster

Country	Period	Title / Description
Bangladesh	March 2013 to March 2015	**Building Parental Capacity to Help Child Nutrition and Health: A Randomized Controlled Trial**
		Researchers will evaluate low-cost integrated interventions, which will combine nutrition with child stimulation for pregnant women and parents with children under the age of three.
Colombia	June 2013 to December 2014	**Medium-Term Effects of a Home-based Early Childhood Development Intervention in Colombia**
		Researchers will evaluate the medium-term effects of a home-based early childhood development intervention that seeks to improve nutrition and development in the first two years of life through home visits to encourage children's psychosocial development and use of micronutrient supplements.
Djibouti	December 2011 to June 2015	**Piloting the First Integrated Nutrition/Workfare Social Safety Net in Djibouti**
		Researchers will examine the effectiveness of linking child nutrition and workfare as a means to reducing malnutrition in very young children.
Gambia	January 2013 to June 2014	**Impact of Supplemental Feeding During Pregnancy on Schooling and Cognitive Development through Adolescence**
		Researchers will assess the impact of the supplemental feeding on the children's schooling decisions and performance.
India	November 2013 to July 2017	**Making Integration the Operative Concept in the Indian Integrated Child Development Strategy**
		Researchers will measure the cost and impact of nutrition services and child stimulation in low-income settings by evaluating a package of services currently being offered to the youngest children in a nationwide child development program.
Indonesia	November 2012 to June 2016	**Early Childhood Nutrition, Availability of Health Service Providers and Life Outcomes as Young Adults: Evidence from Indonesia**
		Researchers will evaluate the effects of the midwife program on the educational decisions and outcomes, cognitive abilities, employment, and life satisfaction of children (who are now young adults) of mothers who had access to midwives.
Madagascar	July 2012 to December 2015	**Addressing Chronic Malnutrition in Madagascar**
		Researchers will conduct a multiarm randomized controlled trial to evaluate the cost-effectiveness of combined interventions designed to tackle chronic malnutrition.
Mozambique	June 2012 to December 2016	**Randomized Impact Evaluation of Integrated early childhood development (ECD) and Intensive Early Nutrition Activities among Vulnerable Communities in Mozambique**
		Researchers will measure the effectiveness of two related programs that provide nutrition, early child stimulation, and parenting information sessions to children, pregnant women, and parents of young children.
Nepal	October 2012 to October 2015	**Evaluating the Impact of Information and "Framed" Unconditional Cash Transfer on Nutritional Outcomes**
		Researchers will evaluate the effectiveness of providing information alone or information and cash on improved nutrition for pregnant women and young children.
Niger	January 2012 to June 2015	**Cash Transfers, Parenting Training and Holistic Early Childhood Development in Niger**
		Researchers will evaluate the effectiveness of cash transfers and of parenting classes on the nutrition, health, and cognitive development of children under the age of 5, and on the health of women of reproductive age.

Source: Strategic Impact Evaluation Fund.
Note: ECD = early childhood development.

Table 6.6 Ongoing SIEF-Funded ECD Impact Evaluations at the World Bank: First Round (2012): Basic Education Service Delivery Cluster

Malawi	October 2011 to August 2014	**Effects of Quality Improvement Strategies on Early Childhood Development in Community-Based Childcare Centers in Malawi: A Randomized Trial**
		Researchers will study the effects of teacher incentives and training, parental education, and learning materials for children on their physical, emotional, and cognitive development and their readiness for primary school.
Bulgaria	June 2013 to June 2014	**Closing the Early Learning Gap between Roma and Non-Roma Children in Bulgaria through Preschool Participation: Inclusive Outreach and (Un)conditional Support Approaches**
		Researchers will measure the effectiveness of a program in more than 150 poor communities that seek to address preschool participation in a variety of ways: encouraging active outreach to parents by local NGOs and authorities, offering free preschool for selected beneficiaries, and providing a conditional financial grant for some selected communities.

Source: Strategic Impact Evaluation Fund.
Note: ECD = early childhood development; NGO = nongovernmental organization.

programs and services. Twelve country diagnostic studies, as well as a regional report benchmarked Middle East and North Africa against other regions in the world, were produced to inform government policy in the region.

In the Pacific Islands, a FY 2012 nonlending TA task is focused on improving learning of children in early education. The work has included a package of advisory services including diagnostics on the foundation of reading skills and early childhood education and development (ECED) services, capacity building to generate data on these areas, and policy dialogue and dissemination of results to produce evidence-based reforms to improve reading skills and ECED services.

In 2010, a capacity-building and TA task for Zambia was implemented to support the implementation of ECD components within the Zambian education sector. Activities included the revision of the ECD curriculum framework, scaling up of capacity building by nongovernmental organizations (NGOs) for training of caregivers, and a report on finance and institutional arrangements for ECD services.

The World Bank's Strategic Impact Evaluation Fund (SIEF) is a multidonor trust fund that supports impact evaluations of innovative programs, capacity building, and knowledge sharing. A new cluster within SIEF is focused on early childhood nutrition, health, and development and supports innovative impact evaluations to expand the evidence base on effective, quality, and scalable interventions. Research priorities include the adoption of a holistic approach for the first 1,000 days of life and understanding the effectiveness and sustainability of at-scale programs. Under its first call for proposals SIEF supported 10 ongoing ECD evaluations through its Early Childhood Nutrition, Health, and Development cluster (see table 6.5) and two through its Basic Education Service Delivery cluster (see table 6.6). Under its second call for proposals in FY 2014, SIEF has recently approved support of six new evaluations through both clusters (see table A.2 in appendix A). When available (some already are), the results of those impact evaluations will help inform future ECD policy and projects not only for the World Bank and its client countries but also for the broader development community.

In addition to AAA, Global Programs and Partnerships related to ECD provide a vehicle for collaboration with development partners to strengthen ECD policies and programs around the world. For example, in FY 2004, the World Bank partnered with other international development agencies, including the Christian Children's Fund, the Arab Resource Collective, International Step by Step Association, Johnson and Johnson Institute, Education Action International, and the National Council of Education in Peru, to implement a worldwide initiative to strengthen the capacity of local ECD trainers and professionals and support the development of community-based ECD programs around the world. More recently, support has been provided in the form of a three-year grant from the Development Grant Facility to the Consultative Group on Early Childhood Care and Development, a global interagency consortium with strong links to regional networks and a track record of advocacy and knowledge generation and dissemination on ECD.

Note

1. As noted in the case of the analysis of commitments for operations, it is important to assess trends in real terms, given that the cumulative impact of inflation for the period as a whole was at about 30 percent for the United States.

CHAPTER 7

Recent Initiatives

Abstract

While the Bank has made substantial investments in early childhood development (ECD) across regions and sectors, and the investments in 2012 and 2013 suggest an upward trend, some challenges to increasing ECD investments still exist. In looking forward, it is important to consider these challenges as well as strategies to address them in order to expand investments in the future. There are several ongoing new initiatives that promote innovative approaches to ECD. The chapter first briefly presents barriers to increased spending that were identified in the portfolio review. It then presents several recent global, regional, and country-specific approaches that address these challenges. These initiatives demonstrate how the World Bank is doing things differently and can hopefully convey a sense of optimism for the future.

What Are the Challenges to Increasing Investment in ECD?

A strong evidence base has emerged that confirms the impact of reaching children during the early years. Bank colleagues and partners no longer lack knowledge in terms of *why* to invest, but rather *how* to invest. As discussed in chapter 5, ECD operations can be complex to implement. This is a challenge both within the Bank and within the country at the levels of policy planning and implementation. There are limited examples of "what works" at scale. While there is a growing knowledge base about successful pilot interventions, there is a need for pilots and impact evaluations to be carried out in the context of scalability and sustainability.

In the context of scarce resources, client countries, and Bank staff are not always willing to prioritize investments in ECD. In the education sector, for example, Bank staff tend to be general education specialists with large work programs and competing priorities for their time and financial allocations. There is a constant pressure from development partners, local education groups, citizens, clients, and Bank management to focus on improving the quality of basic education and, increasingly, to focus on secondary and postsecondary education, including skills and technical vocational education and training (TVET). In the health and nutrition sector, Bank staff may focus on the ECD-aged population, but do not necessarily consider their work to be in "ECD," but, rather, in child health or nutrition. This unfortunately creates missed opportunities for collaboration across sectors. While the evidence is clear that integration is a cost-effective strategy, there are only few examples in the Bank portfolio of nutrition projects that include an early stimulation/parenting component or education projects that reach children or their parents before age four or five.

ECD may have been seen in the past as a "softer" technical area that has not been a focus of World Bank practitioners. ECD is often viewed as an area that other organizations, such as United Nations Children's Fund (UNICEF) and nongovernmental organizations (NGOs), are more likely to fund. While excellent work is being done by these organizations, current global financing levels are inadequate. There is a need for increased cooperation between agencies and programming that is sustainable and planned and executed in a systematic way, without being jeopardized by changes in political priorities.

Governments do not prioritize investment in ECD. The Bank responds to client demand and often governments do not demand ECD. Given that the returns to investment in ECD are longer term, it is difficult for governments to politically prioritize ECD investment. In addition, many countries do not yet have well-developed ECD services that are ready to be rapidly expanded. It is easier to continue to invest in a country's often more developed basic education system than to scale ECD services.

New Initiatives and Opportunities to Expand ECD Investments

SABER-ECD

Building upon the Education Strategy 2020, the Education practice launched the Systems Approach for Better Education Results (SABER) to help countries systematically examine their education policies. Within this initiative, specific education policy domains have been identified to cover the span of education systems from early childhood to entry into the workforce. The ECD domain within SABER is a diagnostic tool that helps policy makers in identifying gaps and areas in need of policy attention to promote healthy and robust development for all children. SABER-ECD supports policy makers and World Bank staff better understand how countries address similar policy challenges related to ECD systems. The SABER-ECD initiative is designed to present participating countries with a holistic multisectoral assessment of the programs and policies which affect young children's development. The SABER-ECD framework (Neuman and Devercelli 2013) presents three core ECD policy goals: *Establishing an Enabling Environment, Implementing Widely*, and *Monitoring and Assuring Quality*. For each policy goal, based on evidence from impact evaluations and a benchmarking exercise of top-performing systems, a set of policy levers are presented that decision makers can act upon in order to strengthen ECD. These policy goals and levers address the range of issues that generally constrain ECD outcomes and

Figure 7.1 SABER-ECD Policy Goals and Levers

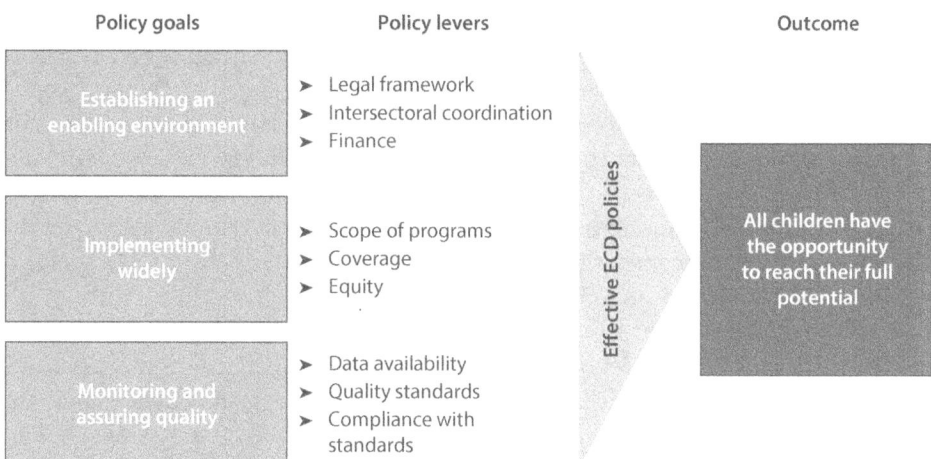

Source: Neuman and Devercelli 2013.
Note: SABER-ECD = Systems Approach for Better Education Results - early childhood development.

form a coherent package that all countries should address to improve ECD outcomes and services. Figure 7.1 presents the conceptual framework of SABER-ECD, displaying the three policy goals and nine related policy levers.

The first policy goal in the tool—*Establishing an Enabling Environment*—is the foundation for effective ECD policies. A country's enabling environment can encourage diverse participation and service uptake, promote efficient service delivery, and ensure adequate financing and institutional capacity. In the context of ECD, establishing an enabling environment entails developing an adequate legal and regulatory framework to support ECD provision. Coordination within sectors and across institutions is necessary to ensure effective service delivery. Finally, the availability of adequate fiscal resources and systems to allocate financing will determine the extent to which the enabling environment supports the ECD system.

The second policy goal—*Implementing Widely*—refers to the coverage and scope of the programs offered and the extent to which access to these programs is equitable. While developing countries have expanded access to preschool provision in the past decade, many still face the challenge of how to take small pilot interventions to scale. Beyond coverage, implementing widely also refers to the scope of the programs offered and the extent to which children's holistic development is addressed through existing interventions. A robust ECD system should include policies that support programs in all essential sectors and target all groups (for example, pregnant women, infants and toddlers, preschoolers, and caregivers). Finally, particular attention must be paid to children from disadvantaged and minority backgrounds as well as those with special needs, so that all children have equitable access to the programs being offered.

The third policy goal—*Monitoring and Assuring Quality*—is also essential. Under political and budget pressures, policy makers may expand access to ECD services at the expense of quality. This may jeopardize the very benefits that policy makers hope children will gain through preschool and other ECD interventions. Impact evaluations suggest that the benefits from ECD interventions may be large, but if programs are not of high quality, the benefits may be negligible and the programs may even be detrimental. Furthermore, in many countries, a large proportion of ECD services are provided by the private sector; for these systems, well-defined and enforced monitoring and quality assurance systems are critical to ensure that standards for service delivery are met. The goal of monitoring and assuring quality refers to the data availability and systems to monitor ECD outcomes, the development of quality standards for ECD service delivery, and systems to monitor compliance with established standards.

The SABER-ECD tool is an instrument to collect data on each of the three policy goals and policy levers, so that an overall assessment of a country's policies can be prepared. Over the last few years, the tool has been implemented in more than 40 countries, and additional countries are being added to the sample. While the tool is not country specific, it has been used to inform policies at the country level. One example is that of Jamaica where SABER-ECD was used by the Early Childhood Commission to inform the drafting of its new National Strategic Plan as well as its national multisector ECD policy. The SABER-ECD analysis helped identify a gap in opportunities for children in the 0–3-year age group, and the country's new ECD Policy and National Strategic Plan for ECD now incorporate a stronger focus on the first 1,000 days. The results from the tool were also used by Bank staff to inform a new ECD project for Jamaica.

A second example of use of the SABER-ECD tool is that of Uganda where the analysis identified a number of existing gaps in the enabling environment for the provision of quality ECD services and bottlenecks in the existing service delivery system in Uganda. This analysis is now informing support provided by the Global Partnership for Education for ECD in Uganda, with a focus on the provision of quality early childhood education services.

A third example is that of Uzbekistan. Subsequent to the initial SABER-ECD analysis which identified gaps in the equitable provision of early childhood care and education (ECCE) services, the government requested an in-depth policy note on ECD whose findings were used to inform the design of a $20.7 million component on early childhood care and education in a Global Partnership for Education (GPE) project to improve access to quality early childhood education opportunities.

Education Staff Development Program

The Education Staff Development Program (ESDP) aims to familiarize Bank staff, partners, and government counterparts with the evidence, technical resources, and best practices related to various investments. The ECD module of the ESDP serves as a resource to increase policy prioritization of ECD. The objective of the ECD-ESDP module is for participants from across education sector (ED), health, nutrition, and population (HNP) sector, and social protection (SP) sector to learn how to design and implement successful ECD policies and programs in low- and middle-income countries. The course brings together theory, practice, and shared experiences so that participants can (i) engage in informed policy dialogue and decision making; (ii) analyze, formulate, critique, and evaluate projects and activities to support ECD; (iii) become familiar with good practices in ECD; and (iv) learn how and when to seek technical support and resources. Between 2012 and 2013, more than 150 Bank staff, development partners, and government counterparts participated in the two-day face-to-face training in Washington, Sydney, and Jakarta. An eLearning version of the course is now available (Wang et al. 2014). The eLearning module course builds on the face-to-face trainings implemented over the last two years and provides approximately four to five hours of learning time (see table 7.1).

ECD Policy Guide

The World Bank's recent ECD policy guide serves as a tool for policy makers to prioritize ECD investments. In 2014, the World Bank produced an ECD policy guide, *Stepping Up Early Childhood Development: Investing in Young Children with High Returns* (Denboba et al. 2014) to outline what countries could and should do to promote ECD. It presents 25 essential ECD interventions, which can be organized in five basic packages; the first four of which are age specific and one that is necessary throughout the ECD period (see figure 7.2).

Table 7.1 eLearning Course on ECD for Policy makers and Practitioners

Introduction: Short animation– "A tale of two girls"

Description: The animation tells about the lives of two girls living in two countries with very different ECD policies and how this affects their development as children as well as their chances later in life.

Module 1: Why invest in ECD?

Description: The module outlines four critical domains of development: physical, cognitive, linguistic, and socio-emotional and reviews the scientific and economic arguments in favor of ECD investments.

Module 2: What matters for ECD?

Description: The module is devoted to a description of a policy diagnostic tool for ECD developed under the SABER framework. The focus is on three policy goals that matter most for effective ECD systems: (1) Establishing an Enabling Environment; (2) Implementing Widely; and (3) Monitoring and Assuring Quality.

Module 3: How to implement ECD interventions?

Description: The last module is the longest and it includes six topics: The first topic provides a summary of findings from this review of the World Bank's experience with ECD projects. The second topic focuses on the importance of intersectoral coordination in ECD policies and programs. The third topic is devoted to ECD diagnostics, whether for countries or projects. The fourth topic is devoted to assessment tools used to monitor child growth and development, and it also includes a brief discussion of impact evaluations. The fifth topic looks at the costs and financing of ECD interventions. Guidelines as to how much a country should invest in ECD programs are also provided with examples of combinations of funding sources, allocation mechanisms, and coverage rates for different types of ECD interventions. The last topic presents discusses issues related to project design, implementation, and monitoring and evaluation. The concepts of results chain and results framework are introduced.

Source: Wang et al. 2014.
Note: ECD = early childhood development; SABER = Systems Approach for Better Education Results.

Figure 7.2 Five Packages of Essential ECD Services and Interventions

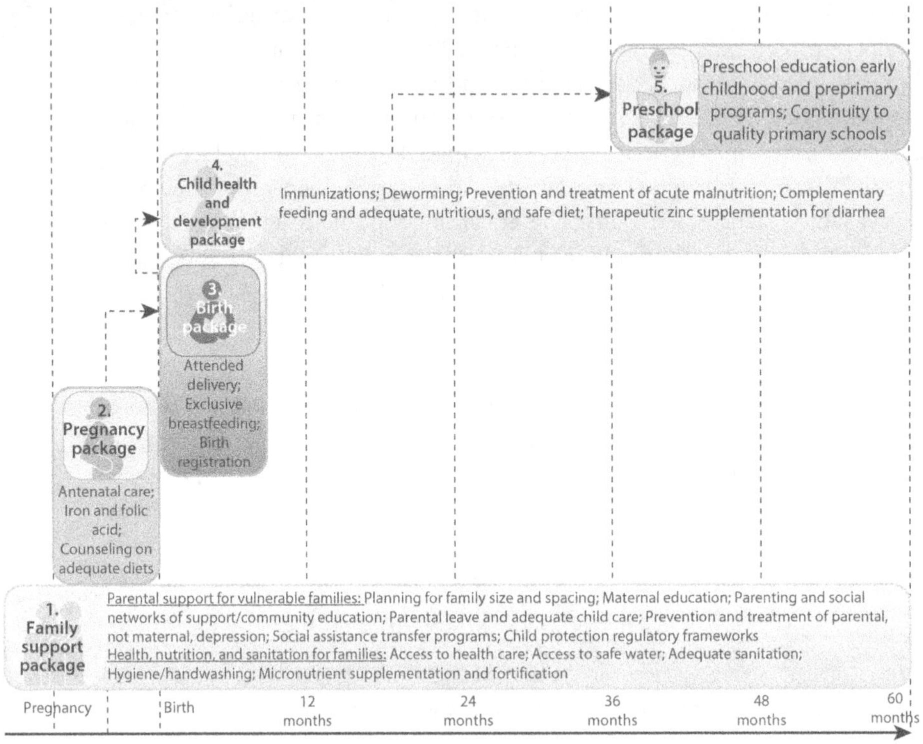

5. Preschool package: Preschool education early childhood and preprimary programs; Continuity to quality primary schools

4. Child health and development package: Immunizations; Deworming; Prevention and treatment of acute malnutrition; Complementary feeding and adequate, nutritious, and safe diet; Therapeutic zinc supplementation for diarrhea

3. Birth package: Attended delivery; Exclusive breastfeeding; Birth registration

2. Pregnancy package: Antenatal care; Iron and folic acid; Counseling on adequate diets

1. Family support package: Parental support for vulnerable families: Planning for family size and spacing; Maternal education; Parenting and social networks of support/community education; Parental leave and adequate child care; Prevention and treatment of parental, not maternal, depression; Social assistance transfer programs; Child protection regulatory frameworks
Health, nutrition, and sanitation for families: Access to health care; Access to safe water; Adequate sanitation; Hygiene/handwashing; Micronutrient supplementation and fortification

Pregnancy | Birth | 12 months | 24 months | 36 months | 48 months | 60 months

Source: Denboba et al. 2014.
Note: ECD = early childhood development.

While these interventions can be delivered by individual sectors, packaging several interventions together can often be more efficient and it may yield greater impact. The entry points to influence young children's development are diverse and involve multiple stakeholders. Interventions in a variety of sectors and areas affect ECD outcomes, including health care and hygiene, nutrition, education, child protection, social protection, and poverty alleviation. Given the holistic needs of young children and the variety of settings and services in which these needs can be met, thinking multisectorally in policy design and coordinating interventions between stakeholders is key to ensure effective and comprehensive ECD service delivery. The ECD Policy Guide outlines four key principles that can help countries design and implement strong ECD policies and programs. Countries should (i) prepare a multisectoral ECD diagnostic and strategy; (ii) implement widely through effective coordination mechanisms established; (iii) create synergies and cost savings among interventions; and finally (iv) monitor, evaluate, and scale up successful interventions.

Early Learning Partnership

The Early Learning Partnership (ELP) is a regional initiative in the Africa region to promote scalable, sustainable, and impactful approaches to supporting young children's development and early learning. The World Bank, with support from partners, including the Children's Investment Fund Foundation, launched the ELP in October 2012 to provide targeted technical assistance and funding to support ECD and early learning across Sub-Saharan Africa. The ELP aims to catalyze change in countries to promote high-quality ECD and early learning opportunities for young children. Strategic goals include mobilizing African governments to prioritize ECD, accelerating the World Bank's financial and operational commitment to ECD, promoting strong partnerships and innovative approaches, and raising the profile of ECD on the global development agenda.

The ELP team works to address issues of regional relevance and by strategically supporting World Bank Task Teams throughout the Africa region. In addition, the ELP issues periodic calls for proposals (roughly one per year) to invite World Bank Task Team Leaders (TTLs) to apply for funding ($20,000–$100,000) to support ECD within their work programs—this funding is intended to leverage significantly larger amounts of finance and impact. A first funding round was awarded in January 2013 and a second in November, 2013. Through the two rounds, a total of $850,000 has been awarded in grants—these initial investments have leveraged more than $17 million in new funding for ECD, mostly through new projects financed by the Global Partnership for Education and the International Development Association. Examples of activities include the development of preschool pilot within the Sierra Leone Global Partnership for Education (GPE) project, the production of the first national ECD strategy and costed implementation plan in Sudan, and the incorporation of parenting education into a cash transfer project in Niger being implemented in 1,500 villages.

The ELP supports awareness raising, sensitization and knowledge sharing in Africa. The ELP cohosted two regional ECD workshops with GPE, UNICEF, and United Nations Educational, Scientific, and Cultural Organization (UNESCO). The workshops included 180 participants from 20 country delegations and provided an opportunity to learn about countries' needs, promote cross-country knowledge sharing, and bring in experts to provide technical assistance in areas such as quality provision, financing, coordination, and measurement. In an effort to connect countries and share information, the ELP has initiated a monthly "virtual panel discussions" series, which uses webinar and audio and video conference technology to connect practitioners and policy makers from around Africa to share promising practices.

To promote continued partnership in investing in ECD in Africa, the ELP coordinates activities and aligns strategies with UNICEF, GPE, and UNESCO within the Africa region. Ongoing discussions with bilateral development agencies and a number of private foundations are yielding additional opportunities for collaboration.

Country-Specific Strategies
In addition to global initiatives and partnerships within the World Bank, there have also been several recent country-specific strategies to respond to client needs in order to expand ECD investments. Experience in Mozambique presents an excellent example where government officials and other stakeholders

have received targeted training in relevant ECD issues. In order to strengthen the Government of Mozambique's implementation capacity to support ECD service delivery in the country, the Ministry of Education (supported by a Bank-funded ECD operation) will offer a series of eight trainings over the course of two years to government officials and other stakeholders (including development partners and civil society organizations) involved in the $40 million ECD operation being implemented with IDA financing. Trainings will cover topics such as the following: A General Introduction to ECD, Community Sensitization and Mobilization, Monitoring and Evaluation (M&E) of ECD, Program Management, and Quality Standards of ECD.

In June 2013, during five days, the first series—Introduction to ECD—was delivered to approximately 60 stakeholders (including those from the Ministry of Education, the Ministry of Health, the Ministry of Women and Social Affairs, the Ministry of Justice, other government agencies contributing to the implementation of the project, and a range of civil society organizations and development partners active in the field of ECD). Participants came from national, provincial, and district levels. The training was facilitated by an international ECD expert with the support of national ECD specialists and included active participation, hands-on activities, simulations and role-play. Some of the challenges in implementing the training so far have included the following: (i) the different levels of ECD-related experiences and knowledge among participants, which at times made it difficult for facilitators to actively engage all participants and (ii) the fact that key government staff from provincial and district level could not participate in this first training due to delays in their recruitment and contracting. Despite these challenges, however, the training was well received and helped establish a strong foundation in ECD among participants. The remaining seven trainings will build upon this first experience and incorporate lessons learned

Conclusion

The increase in number of investments in ECD from 2011 to 13 reflects a growing demand from clients in all regions to address the needs of young children. With a growing portfolio of analytical work, the Bank is increasing its knowledge base of ECD systems and interventions. In addition, recent initiatives, including Strategic Impact Evaluation Fund (SIEF), SABER-ECD, the ECD component of the Education Staff Development Program, and the ELP for the Africa Region have the potential to expand partnerships, innovate new approaches, and inform new investment priorities. Taking advantage of—and expanding upon—gained knowledge and experience will allow the Bank and its partners to ensure that young children throughout the world are provided with the opportunity to lead happy, healthy, and productive lives.

APPENDIX A

Supporting Figures and Tables

Table A.1 Investment in ECD Per Country, Per Person, and Per Poor Person, FY 2001 to FY 2011

	Number of IBRD/ IDA projects	Investment (US$ million) (US$ of 2013)	ECD investment per child under 5 (US$ of 2013)	ECD investment per child under 5 in poverty (US$) [poverty as $1.25 per day]
Panama	5	54.46	13.44	203.65
Djibouti	4	15.33	13.40	71.28
Argentina	3	448.12	12.04	1,204.00
Bulgaria	1	42.39	11.32	1,132.02
Haiti	1	90.00	6.59	10.69
Dominican Republic	2	73.56	6.26	284.53
Jamaica	1	16.16	5.96	596.36
Lebanon	1	16.26	5.42	—
Eritrea	1	51.07	4.71	—
Lesotho	1	12.00	4.31	9.92
Uruguay	1	10.53	3.88	388.48
Central African Republic	1	26.94	3.79	6.04
Honduras	3	38.13	3.57	19.97
Sri Lanka	2	69.32	3.40	82.90
Burundi	3	55.19	2.98	3.66
Romania	2	33.33	2.75	275.31
Malawi	1	81.32	2.71	3.66
Bolivia	3	36.56	2.64	16.89
Grenada	1	0.28	2.59	—
Senegal	4	59.12	2.46	8.30
Jordan	2	22.80	2.41	240.54
Guatemala	1	55.47	2.33	17.29
Afghanistan	6	125.13	2.26	3.77
Nepal	4	76.12	2.18	8.78
Benin	2	34.20	1.98	4.18

table continues next page

Table A.1 Investment in ECD Per Country, Per Person, and Per Poor Person, FY 2001 to FY 2011 *(continued)*

	Number of IBRD/ IDA projects	Investment (US$ million) (US$ of 2013)	ECD investment per child under 5 (US$ of 2013)	ECD investment per child under 5 in poverty (US$) [poverty as $1.25 per day]
Colombia	2	95.07	1.91	23.34
Angola	1	74.65	1.79	3.29
Congo, Dem. Rep.	3	208.20	1.69	1.93
Mozambique	2	77.66	1.66	2.79
Yemen, Rep.	2	59.04	1.61	9.18
Mexico	4	203.32	1.60	159.71
Guinea	2	31.21	1.59	3.67
Madagascar	4	56.00	1.51	1.85
Peru	4	44.09	1.37	27.89
Vietnam	1	100.00	1.26	7.44
Armenia	2	2.87	1.21	48.31
Brazil	3	157.81	0.94	15.47
Mauritania	1	5.57	0.92	3.91
Ethiopia	2	137.24	0.90	2.94
Ghana	1	26.93	0.69	2.43
Kyrgyz Republic	2	3.77	0.58	8.60
Lao PDR	1	5.21	0.56	1.66
Timor-Leste	1	1.08	0.54	—
Nigeria	1	152.47	0.49	0.73
Uganda	1	31.63	0.44	1.15
Indonesia	1	105.05	0.38	2.10
Mali	2	10.82	0.37	0.73
Nicaragua	2	2.47	0.33	2.77
Ecuador	1	5.50	0.31	6.83
Egypt, Arab Rep.	2	25.45	0.26	25.93
Azerbaijan	1	1.72	0.22	22.16
Turkey	1	14.55	0.21	20.80
Togo	1	2.03	0.18	0.64
Chad	1	4.56	0.18	0.29
Cambodia	1	2.46	0.14	0.76
Bangladesh	1	23.66	0.14	0.32
Burkina Faso	1	4.23	0.14	0.31
India	2	108.45	0.08	0.25
Pakistan	1	18.89	0.08	0.38
Morocco	1	2.63	0.08	3.21
Kenya	1	2.11	0.03	0.07

Source: World Bank data.
Note: ECD = Early Childhood Development; FY = fiscal year; IBRD = International Bank for Reconstruction and Development; IDA = International Development Association; — = not available.

Supporting Figures and Tables

Map A.1 Distribution of HD IBRD/IDA ECD Commitments Per Child under Five

[World map showing distribution with legend: 6.0 and above; 2.0–5.9; 1.0–1.9; 0.9 and below]

Source: World Bank data.

Table A.2 New Ongoing SIEF-Funded Impact Evaluations at the World Bank: Second Round, 2013

Early Childhood Nutrition, Development and Health Cluster	**1. Burkina Faso:** Impact evaluation of the ECD and nutrition component of Burkina Faso's safety net project
	2. Mali: Impact and cost-effectiveness of an integrated parenting, nutrition, and malaria prevention package to improve nutrition and early child development in infants and preschool children (0–6 years): A randomized controlled trial in southern Mali
	3. India: An impact and process evaluation of the use of women's self-help groups to catalyze and strengthen convergence of health, nutrition, sanitation, and food security programs in rural Bihar, India
	4. India: Early childhood development for the poor: Evaluating the impacts
	5. India: SPRING: linking implementation strength, outcomes, and lessons learned to inform scale up
Basic Ed Service Delivery Cluster	**6. Sierra Leone:** Comparing approaches to preprimary school provision in Sierra Leone

Source: Strategic Impact Evaluation Fund (SIEF).
Note: ECD = early childhood development.

APPENDIX B

Human Development ECD Project Portfolio

B.1 Operations (Lending and Trust Funded)

A. Self-Standing Operations

Project ID	Project name	Product line	Country	TTL	Lending instrument	Approval date	Total project cost	Total invested on ECD (in US$ million, nominal)	Total invested on ECD (in US$ million, US$ of 2013)
Education									
P068463	Integrated Early Childhood Development Project	IBRD/IDA	Eritrea	Hirshberg, Susan E.	SIL	FY01	45.00	40.00	51.07
TF038620	UGANDA: NUTRITION and EARLY CHILDHOOD DEVELOPMENT PROJECT	SF (bank executed)	Uganda	Carla Bertoncino		FY01	0.03	0.03	0.04
TF038622	KENYA: EARLY CHILDHOOD DEVELOPMENT PROJECT	SF (bank executed)	Kenya	Carla Bertoncino		FY02	0.02	0.02	0.02
TF038627	KENYA: EARLY CHILDHOOD DEVELOPMENT PROJECT	SF (bank executed)	Kenya	Carla Bertoncino		FY02	0.02	0.02	0.02
TF038633	ERITREA: INTEGRATED EARLY CHILDHOOD DEVELOPMENT PROGRAM	SF (bank executed)	Eritrea	Christine Lao Pena		FY02	0.02	0.02	0.02
TF038986	KENYA—EARLY CHILDHOOD DEVELOPMENT AND PRIMARY AND SECONDARY ED PROJECTS	SF (bank executed)	Kenya	Carla Bertoncino		FY02	0.02	0.02	0.02
TF040199	UGANDA: NUTRITION AND EARLY CHILDHOOD DEVELOPMENT	SF (bank executed)	Uganda	Carla Bertoncino		FY02	0.02	0.02	0.02
TF040230	KENYA: EARLY CHILDHOOD DEVELOPMENT PROJECT	SF (bank executed)	Kenya	Adriana Jaramillo		FY02	0.01	0.01	0.02
P054937	Early Childhood ED Project	IBRD/IDA	Dominican Republic	McEvoy, Karla J.	SIL	FY03	62.00	42.00	51.75
TF050949	JSDF-GUINEA(WEST AFRICA):STRATEGIC ALLIANCE FOR GRASSROOTS CAPACITY BUILDING IN EARLY CHILDHOOD DEVELOPMENT	REA	Guinea	Michael Drabble		FY03	0.02	0.02	0.03

table continues next page

A. Self-Standing Operations (continued)

Project ID	Project name	Product line	Country	TTL	Lending instrument	Approval date	Total project cost	Total invested on ECD (in US$ million, nominal)	Total invested on ECD (in US$ million, US$ of 2013)
TF050948	JSDF-GUINEA(WEST AFRICA): STRATEGIC ALLIANCE FOR GRASSROOTS CAPACITY BUILDING IN EARLY CHILDHOOD DEVELOPMENT	REA	Guinea	Michael Drabble		FY04	0.43	0.43	0.52
TF051548	JSDF-MALI(WEST AFRICA): STRATEGIC ALLIANCE FOR GRASSROOTS CAPACITY BUILDING IN EARLY CHILDHOOD DEVELOPMENT	REA	Mali	William Experton		FY04	0.28	0.28	0.33
TF051549	JSDF-MALI(WEST AFRICA):STRATEGIC ALLIANCE FOR GRASSROOTS CAPCITY BUILDING IN EARLY CHILDHOOD DEVELOPMENT	REA	Mali	William Experton		FY04	0.01	0.01	0.01
P082952	Early Childhood ED Enhancement Project (ECEEP)	IBRD/IDA	Egypt, Arab Rep.	Gamal El Din, Mahmoud	SIL	FY05	108.62	19.59	22.91
TF052939	JSDF-VIETNAM: EARLY CHILDHOOD CARE AND DEVELOPMENT	REA	Vietnam	Binh Thanh Vu	SIL	FY05	1.91	1.91	2.23
P089479	Early Childhood ED and Development Project	IBRD/IDA	Indonesia	Roesli, Rosfita	SIL	FY06	127.74	92.80	105.05
P101439	ED for All, Fast Track Initiative Catalytic Fund for Moldova	REA	Moldova	Moarcas, Mariana Doina	SIL	FY06	4.40	4.40	4.98
P095673	Jamaica Early Childhood Development Project	IBRD/IDA	Jamaica	Nannyonjo, Harriet	SIL	FY08	508.87	15.00	16.16
P124612	Piloting Effective Early Childhood Development Services in Mali	REA	Mali	Premand, Patrick	LIL	FY11	2.00	2.00	2.07
P118423	Fast Track Initiative Catalytic Grant Fund -2	REA	Kyrgyz Republic	Hou, Dingyong	SIL	FY11	6.00	6.00	6.21

table continues next page

A. Self-Standing Operations *(continued)*

Project ID	Project name	Product line	Country	TTL	Lending instrument	Approval date	Total project cost	Total invested on ECD (in US$ million, nominal)	Total invested on ECD (in US$ million, US$ of 2013)
P124729	MZ—AF to Education Sector Support Project	IBRD/IDA	Mozambique	Naudeau, Sophie	SIL	FY12	40.00	40.00	40.66
P125445	Mongolia Global Partnership for Education Early Childhood Education Project	REA	Mongolia	Tandon, Prateek	SIL	FY12	10.00	10.00	10.16
P130580	BO Early Childhood Care and Development in the Poorest and Most Vulnerable Urban Districts of La Paz and El Alto	REA	Bolivia	Alvarez, Patricia	TAL	FY12	2.79	2.79	2.84
P117393	Vietnam School Readiness Promotion Project	IBRD/IDA	Vietnam	Stevens, James A.	SIL	FY13	100.00	100.00	100.00
Health, Nutrition, and Population									
P070541	Nutrition Enhancement Program	IBRD/IDA	Senegal	Mulder-Sibanda, Menno	APL	FY02	20.20	14.70	18.44
TF038653	PHILIPPINES: EARLY CHILDHOOD DEVELOPMENT PROJECT	SF (bank executed)	Philippines	Teresa Ho		FY02	0.01	0.01	0.01
P084601	Madagascar: Nutrition II—Supplemental Credit	IBRD/IDA	Madagascar	Sharp, Maryanne	SIL	FY04	11.00	10.00	12.05
TF024927	ERITREA INTEGRATED EARLY CHILDHOOD DEVELOPMENT	REA	Eritrea	Christopher D. Walker		FY04	5.00	5.00	6.02
P065126	Health Sector Support Project	IBRD/IDA	Guinea	Magazi, Ibrahim	SIL	FY05	27.80	25.00	29.24

table continues next page

A. Self-Standing Operations *(continued)*

Project ID	Project name	Product line	Country	TTL	Lending instrument	Approval date	Total project cost	Total invested on ECD (in US$ million, nominal)	Total invested on ECD (in US$ million, US$ of 2013)
P090137	GAIN National Food Fortification Program	REA	Morocco	Maeda, Akiko	SIL	FY05	35.63	2.92	3.42
P077756	GUATEMALA Maternal and Infant Health and Nutrition	IBRD/IDA	Guatemala	Pena, Christine Lao	SIL	FY06	49.00	49.00	55.47
P103712	Reproductive and Child Health—Phase I	REA	Sierra Leone	Rose, Laura L.	SIL	FY07	6.00	6.00	6.60
P105092	Nutrition and Malaria Control for Child Survival	IBRD/IDA	Ghana	Awittor, Evelyn	SIL	FY08	25.50	25.00	26.93
P104946	Yemen, Rep. Safe Motherhood Voucher Program	REA	Yemen, Rep.	Abdel-Hamid, Alaa Mahmoud Hamed	SIL	FY08	6.50	6.50	7.00
P112136	Community and Basic Health Addl Financing	SF (bank executed)	Tajikistan	Jaganjac, Nedim	ERL	FY08	4.00	4.00	4.31
P104794	Health Sector Strategic Plan Support Project	IBRD/IDA	Timor-Leste	Lee, Yi-Kyoung	SIL	FY08	20.30	1.00	1.08
P101160	Health Sector Development Support	IBRD/IDA	Burundi	Rajkumar, Andrew Sunil	SIL	FY09	25.00	25.00	26.50
P115938	Rapid Response Child-Focused Social Cash Transfer and Nutrition Security Project	IBRD/IDA	Senegal	Mulder-Sibanda, Menno	ERL	FY09	18.00	18.00	19.08
P095563	PE—(APL2) Health Reform Program	IBRD/IDA	Peru	Lavadenz, Fernando	APL	FY09	162.40	15.00	15.90
P131548	Delivering Maternal Child Health Care to Vulnerable Populations in Swaziland	REA	Swaziland	Shelton, Carolyn J.	SIL	FY09	2.57	2.57	2.72
P111840	Municipal Health Service Strengthening (Revitaliza)	IBRD/IDA	Angola	Cossa, Humberto Albino	SIL	FY10	91.80	70.80	74.65

table continues next page

A. Self-Standing Operations *(continued)*

Project ID	Project name	Product line	Country	TTL	Lending instrument	Approval date	Total project cost	Total invested on ECD (in US$ million, nominal)	Total invested on ECD (in US$ million, US$ of 2013)
P113202	Health System Performance	IBRD/IDA	Benin	Lemiere, Christophe	SIL	FY10	33.80	22.80	24.04
P110535	Reproductive and Child Health Project—Phase 2	REA	Sierra Leone	Awittor, Evelyn	SIL	FY10	20.00	20.00	21.09
P122244	TJ—JSDF Grant for a Nutrition Pilot	REA	Tajikistan	Msisha, Wezi Marianne	TAL	FY10	2.80	2.80	2.95
P114863	Community Nutrition Project	SF (bank executed)	Lao PDR	Tandon, Ajay	ERL	FY10	2.00	2.00	2.11
P094755	Yemen, Rep. Health and Population	IBRD/IDA	Yemen, Rep.	Abdel-Hamid, Alaa Mahmoud Hamed	SIL	FY11	37.00	35.00	36.25
P124191	Benin Community Nutrition	REA	Benin	Mulder-Sibanda, Menno	SIL	FY11	2.80	2.80	2.90
P121509	Gambia Rapid Response Nutrition Security Improvement Project	REA	Gambia	Mulder-Sibanda, Menno	ERL	FY11	3.00	3.00	3.11
P120495	Community Nutrition Project EU Funding	REA	Lao PDR	Tandon, Ajay	ERL	FY11	2.12	2.12	2.20
P125237	Malawi Nutrition and HIV/AIDS Project	IBRD/IDA	Malawi	Clark, John Paul	SIL	FY12	80.00	80.00	81.32
P129398	Additional Financing Nutrition Enhancement Project (PRN2)	IBRD/IDA	Senegal	Mulder-Sibanda, Menno	APL	FY12	10.00	10.00	10.16
P120798	Nigeria States Health Investment Project	IBRD/IDA	Nigeria	Odutolu, Ayodeji Oluwole	SIL	FY12	150.00	150.00	152.47
P125359	Nepal: Community Action for Nutrition Project (Sunaula Hazar Din)	IBRD/IDA	Nepal	Bhattarai, Manav	SIL	FY12	40.00	40.00	40.66

table continues next page

A. Self-Standing Operations (continued)

Project ID	Project name	Product line	Country	TTL	Lending instrument	Approval date	Total project cost	Total invested on ECD (in US$ million, nominal)	Total invested on ECD (in US$ million, US$ of 2013)
P119815	CF-Health System Support Project	IBRD/IDA	Central African Republic	Sorgho, Gaston	SIL	FY12	17.00	26.50	26.94
P126742	Health Sector Development Support—Additional Financing	REA	Burundi	Zine Eddine El Idrissi, Moulay Driss	SIL	FY12	0.00	45.00	45.74
P129024	Benin—Health System Performance Project—Additional Financing	IBRD/IDA	Benin	Lemiere, Christophe	SIL	FY12	10.00	10.00	10.16
P123706	Improving Maternal and Child Health through Integrated Social Services	IBRD/IDA	Haiti	Rajkumar, Andrew Sunil	SIL	FY13	70.00	90.00	90.00
P121731	India: ICDS Systems Strengthening and Nutrition Improvement Program (ISSNIP)	IBRD/IDA	India	Kathuria, Ashi Kohli	APL	FY13	106.00	106.00	106.00
P125477	Mozambique Nutrition Additional Financing	IBRD/IDA	Mozambique	Hyder, Ziauddin	SIL	FY13	37.00	37.00	37.00
P131919	Second Additional Financing Burundi Health Sector Development Support Project	IBRD/IDA	Burundi	Zine Eddine El Idrissi, Moulay Driss	SIL	FY13	25.00	25.00	25.00
P133329	Strengthen IYCF Capacity in South Asia	REA	South Asia	Kathuria, Ashi Kohli	TAL	FY13	0.00	0.48	0.48
P114859	Lesotho Maternal and Newborn Health PBF	IBRD/IDA	Lesotho	Yamashita-Allen, Kanako	SIL	FY13	12.00	12.00	12.00
P123531	Ethiopia Health MDG Support Operation	IBRD/IDA	Ethiopia	Ramana, Gandham N.V.	P4R	FY13	100.00	120.00	120.00

table continues next page

A. Self-Standing Operations (continued)

Project ID	Project name	Product line	Country	TTL	Lending instrument	Approval date	Total project cost	Total invested on ECD (in US$ million, nominal)	Total invested on ECD (in US$ million, US$ of 2013)
Social Protection									
P100657	Social Inclusion Project	IBRD/IDA	Bulgaria	Pojarski, Peter Ivanov	SIL	FY09	136.73	40.00	42.39
P120888	PERU Participatory intervention model to improve child nutrition	REA	Peru	Marini, Alessandra	TAL	FY10	1.90	1.90	2.01
P117310	Results in Nutrition for Juntos SWAp	IBRD/IDA	Peru	Marini, Alessandra	SIL	FY11	54.00	25.00	25.89
P121496	Protecting Early Childhood Development in Malawi—Rapid Social Response (RSR)	REA	Malawi	Neuman, Michelle J.	TAL	FY11	2.00	2.00	2.07
P121690	Household Development Agent Pilot	REA	Haiti	Lamanna, Francesca	SIL	FY11	1.50	1.50	1.55
P144484	Cash Transfer Program for Vulnerable Children in Northern Togo	REA	Togo	Van Dyck, John	SIL	FY13	0.00	2.55	2.55

table continues next page

B.1 Operations (Lending and Trust Funded)

B. Components of Operations

Project ID	Project name	Component name	Product line	Country	TTL	Lending instrument	Approval date	Total project cost	Total invested on ECD (in US$ million, nominal)	Total invested on ECD (in US$ million, US$ of 2013)
Education										
P052021	Basic ED Project (02)	Comp 2: Expansion of the Nonformal Preschool ED Program	IBRD/IDA	Panama	Bonilla-Chacin, Maria Eugenia	SIL	FY01	59.00	3.10	3.96
P055455	Rajasthan Second District Primary ED Project	Sub comp1.1bi (part of Component 1: expanding access, retention and enrollments)—establishing Early Childhood ED centers	IBRD/IDA	India	Jena, Nalin	SIL	FY01	87.50	1.92	2.45
P007397	Community Based ED Project	Sub Comp (part of Comp 2: Community-based preschool (and basic) ED services), Comp 1: application of national curriculum)	IBRD/IDA	Honduras	Guedes, Andrea C.	SIL	FY01	47.80	15.77	20.13
P040650	ED Sector Expenditure Program	Subcomp 1.a: Early Childhood Development(Under Comp 1—Improving the quality of teaching and learning) Sub Comp 2.a- Extension of Early Childhood Development enters	IBRD/IDA	Mali	Ouedraogo, Adama	APL	FY01	541.20	5.58	7.12

table continues next page

B. Components of Operations (continued)

Project ID	Project name	Component name	Product line	Country	TTL	Lending instrument	Approval date	Total project cost	Total invested on ECD (in US$ million, nominal)	Total invested on ECD (in US$ million, US$ of 2013)
P059566	Ceara Basic ED Quality Improvement Project	Subcomp 1.1.d: Enhancing Teacher Development and Early Childhood Development (ECD) Programs-- expansion of nonformal ECD activities through training of the community Health Agents, who will then train parents and community workers to provide nonformal initial ED	IBRD/IDA	Brazil	Silveira, Ricardo Rocha	SIL	FY01	150.00	4.58	5.84
P050046	ED for All Project	Subcomp 2a:Establishment of an Early Childhood Development program	IBRD/IDA	Guinea	Lahire, Nathalie	APL	FY02	70.00	1.57	1.97
P000309	Basic ED Sector Project	Early Childhood Development (under Component 2: Improving quality and efficiency of basic ED)	IBRD/IDA	Burkina Faso	Ouedraogo, Adama	SIL	FY02	96.20	3.37	4.23
P077896	Emergency ED Rehabilitation and Development Project	Sub Comp 1.2—Literacy Learning and early Childhood Development	IBRD/IDA	Afghanistan	Wajdi, Habibullah	ERL	FY02	15.00	1.00	1.25
P070937	Third Basic ED Quality Improvement Project	Sub. Comp of Comp 1—Expansion of Full-time School Model (Construction of preschools, learning materials for preschools, teacher training for preschools)	IBRD/IDA	Uruguay	Ambasz, Diego	SIL	FY02	56.00	8.40	10.53

table continues next page

B. Components of Operations *(continued)*

Project ID	Project name	Component name	Product line	Country	TTL	Lending instrument	Approval date	Total project cost	Total invested on ECD (in US$ million, nominal)	Total invested on ECD (in US$ million, US$ of 2013)
P057531	Basic ED Development Phase II	Subcomp 1.3.1 Training initial ED staff	IBRD/IDA	Mexico	Patrinos, Harry Anthony	APL	FY02	531.10	40.78	51.14
P071308	ED Sector Development Program	Subcomp1.3: Promoting ECD Activities to Enhance Physical, Socio-emotional and Cognitive Development of Children	IBRD/IDA	Mauritania	Diallo, Cherif	APL	FY02	323.65	4.44	5.57
P055232	Rural ED Project	Subcomp 1.1: Access to Quality Initial and Preschool ED	IBRD/IDA	Peru	Benavides, Livia M.	APL	FY03	94.20	1.45	1.79
P075829	ED Reform for Knowledge Economy I Program	Comp 4: Promote Readiness for Learning though ECE	IBRD/IDA	Jordan	Moreno Olmedilla, Juan Manuel	SIML	FY03	370.00	18.50	22.80
P000527	ED Sector Reform Project	Subcomp 2.5: ECD Program	IBRD/IDA	Chad	Cisse, Boubou	SIL	FY03	119.66	3.70	4.56
P059872	Basic ED 2 Project (APL #2)	Sub comp 1.2: Preschool classroom construction, Sub Comp 2,3. Preschool ED and Nonformal early childhood programs, Sub comp. 3.2: In service training in preschol ED, Sub. Component 3.5: Mother and Child ED	IBRD/IDA	Turkey	McLaughlin, Maureen Anne	APL	FY03	356.86	11.81	14.55

table continues next page

B. Components of Operations *(continued)*

Project ID	Project name	Component name	Product line	Country	TTL	Lending instrument	Approval date	Total project cost	Total invested on ECD (in US$ million, nominal)	Total invested on ECD (in US$ million, US$ of 2013)
P074503	ED Quality and Relevance Project (APL #1)	SubComp: Pilot alternative preschool models for national preschool ED strategy with a view to increase overall enrollment and improve school readiness (Under Component 4)	IBRD/IDA	Armenia	Mulatu, Meskerem	APL	FY04	21.70	0.19	0.23
P074633	ED for All Project	Comp 2: Enhancing quality and relevance. Early Childhood Development (ECD), delivered through community-managed centers and through preprimary classes will be expanded[en]Community-managed centers and through preprimary classes, will be expanded	IBRD/IDA	Nepal	Sundararaman, Venkatesh	SIL	FY05	664.00	5.00	5.85
P043412	Morocco Basic ED Reform Support Program	Subcomp 1.1: Promote preprimary ED through partnership	IBRD/IDA	Morocco	Waite, Jeffrey	SIL	FY05	150.55	2.25	2.63
P078990	NICARAGUA—ED PROJECT	Comp 4: Pilot Program for Community Preschools	IBRD/IDA	Nicaragua	Drabble, Michael	SIL	FY05	15.00	0.12	0.14
P085851	MX Basic ED Dev Phase III	Comp 1: Initial ED	IBRD/IDA	Mexico	Silveira, Ricardo Rocha	APL	FY05	500.00	63.40	74.15

table continues next page

B. Components of Operations *(continued)*

Project ID	Project name	Component name	Product line	Country	TTL	Lending instrument	Approval date	Total project cost	Total invested on ECD (in US$ million, nominal)	Total invested on ECD (in US$ million, US$ of 2013)
P070963	Rural ED Improvement Project (PROMER)	preschool activities under: subcomp A1—improve operating conditions of rural preschool AND Subcomponent A.2 Improve school coverage at the preschool level for 5-year-olds in rural areas	IBRD/IDA	Argentina	Holland, Peter Anthony	SIL	FY06	240.58	40.60	45.96
P087479	ED Sector Support Program	early childhood and development (under policy area 2: enhancing quality and learning achievement)	IBRD/IDA	Kenya	Sosale, Shobhana	SIML	FY07	1354.30	1.92	2.11
P087831	EC-Inclusion and Quality ED	Comp 1: Improvement of Human Resources Management and Coordination for the Provision of Early Childhood ED (ECE).	IBRD/IDA	Ecuador	Benavides, Livia M.	SIL	FY07	43.40	5.00	5.50
P110576	ED For All-Fast Track Initiative Program	Sub Comp of Comp 2: Improve quality of preschool and primary ED and literacy training	REA	Benin	Gbaye, Hyacinthe	SIL	FY07	76.00	17.80	19.59

table continues next page

B. Components of Operations *(continued)*

Project ID	Project name	Component name	Product line	Country	TTL	Lending instrument	Approval date	Total project cost	Total invested on ECD (in US$ million, nominal)	Total invested on ECD (in US$ million, US$ of 2013)
P106451	ED for All Fast Track Initiative Catalytic Fund Grant	Sub components of Comp 1: Improve physical and learning conditions in pre- and primary school and promote community involvement, and Comp 2: Improve Learning Conditions in preschools and primary schools	REA	Kyrgyz Republic	Hou, Dingyong	SIL	FY07	0.00	2.00	2.20
P108776	ED for All Fast Track Initiative Catalytic Fund Grant	Component 2: Improve Preschool ED in rural areas by building mobile gerkindergartens	REA	Mongolia	Prateek Tandon	SIL	FY07	8.29	0.13	0.14
P102117	Second ED Sector Development Project	Comp 4. Promoting School Readiness.	IBRD/IDA	Azerbaijan	Mulatu, Meskerem	APL	FY08	45.40	1.60	1.72
P101218	Honduras ED Quality, Governance, and Institutional Strengthening	Subcomp 1.1: Coverage expansion for preschool education in rural areas	IBRD/IDA	Honduras	Alonso, Juan Diego	SIL	FY08	16.40	4.10	4.42
P105555	Basic ED - Additional Financing	Comp 2: Expansion of Preschool ED.	IBRD/IDA	Panama	Bonilla-Chacin, Maria Eugenia	SIL	FY08	7.00	2.30	2.48

table continues next page

B. Components of Operations *(continued)*

Project ID	Project name	Component name	Product line	Country	TTL	Lending instrument	Approval date	Total project cost	Total invested on ECD (in US$ million, nominal)	Total invested on ECD (in US$ million, US$ of 2013)
P109925	KH–ED FOR ALL FAST TRACK INITIATIVE CATALYTIC TRUST FUND	Comp 1: Expanding Early Childhood ED	REA	Cambodia	Beng, Simeth	SIL	FY08	57.40	14.06	15.15
P107772	Second ED Quality and Relevance (APL 2)	Subcomp 1: Promoting School Readiness and equal opportunities at the start of General ED	IBRD/IDA	Armenia	Aedo Inostroza, Mario Cristian	APL	FY09	31.26	2.49	2.64
P106686	Basic ED Quality Improvement Project	Sub Comp 2.1: Expand access to nonformal ED programs in rural and indigenous areas	IBRD/IDA	Panama	Bonilla-Chacin, Maria Eugenia	SIL	FY09	42.00	9.35	9.91
P115264	Fast Track Initiative Grant for Basic ED	Subcomponents of development objectives: improve access, equity, coverage, quality	REA	Burkina Faso	Ouedraogo, Adama	DPL	FY09	22.00	2.20	2.33
P105036	Second ED Reform for the Knowledge Economy	Subcomponent 4.1: ECD program	IBRD/IDA	Jordan	Moreno Olmedilla, Juan Manuel	SIL	FY09	408.00	0.00	0.00
P115347	School Based Management	1/5 of School Based Management programming included preschools	IBRD/IDA	Mexico	Bentaouet Kattan, Raja	APL	FY10	366.70	44.00	46.39
P101369	Compensatory ED	Early Childhood Development Intervention	IBRD/IDA	Mexico	Holland, Peter Anthony	SIL	FY10	166.70	30.00	31.63

table continues next page

B. Components of Operations *(continued)*

Project ID	Project name	Component name	Product line	Country	TTL	Lending instrument	Approval date	Total project cost	Total invested on ECD (in US$ million, nominal)	Total invested on ECD (in US$ million, US$ of 2013)
P116426	EFA Fast Track Initiative Catalytic Fund Grant for Lesotho	Component 2: Support and contribution to the expansion of preprimary ED	REA	Lesotho	Panasco Santos, Cristina Isabel	SIL	FY10	26.80	1.50	1.58
P115427	The Gambia EFA-FTI Catalytic Fund 2009-2011	Subcomponents of Comp 1 (increasing acces and quity); 2 (improving quality of teaching and learning)	REA	Gambia	Lahire, Nathalie	SIL	FY10	28.00	2.80	2.95
P118187	Second ED Development Project	Comp 1: Early Childhood Education	IBRD/IDA	Lebanon	Moreno Olmedilla, Juan Manuel	SIL	FY11	42.60	15.70	16.26
P117662	Fast Track Initiative Grant for Basic ED		REA	Liberia	Inoue, Keiko	SIL	FY11	40.00	7.20	7.46
P114609	Catalytic Fund EFA/FTI	Sub-comp—of Component 1: Access and Quality for Preprimary and Primary ED Levels and Component 2: School Feeding for Preprimary and Primary ed	REA	Lao PDR	Regel, Omporn	SIL	FY11	50.00	3.00	3.11
P126372	Recife Swap Education and Public Management	Component 1: Strengthen coverage of Early Child Education and create conditions conducive to learning in Primary Education	IBRD/IDA	Brazil	Drabble, Michael	SIL	FY12	130.00	100.00	101.64

table continues next page

B. Components of Operations *(continued)*

Project ID	Project name	Component name	Product line	Country	TTL	Lending instrument	Approval date	Total project cost	Total invested on ECD (in US$ million, nominal)	Total invested on ECD (in US$ million, US$ of 2013)
P130760	Mongolia: Improving Primary Education Outcomes for the most vulnerable children in rural Mongolia	Component 1: strengthening school preparation programs for new school entrants (5–6 years of age) in the community	REA	Mongolia	Chuluun, Tungalag	SIL	FY12	0.00	0.73	0.74
P123151	PE Basic Education		IBRD/IDA	Peru	Kudo, Ines	SIL	FY13	25.00	0.51	0.51
P131945	Madagascar Emergency Support to Critical Education, Health and Nutrition Services Project	Component 2: Preserving Critical Health services ($25 mil) Component 3: Preserving critical nutrition services ($10.5 mil)	IBRD/IDA	Madagascar	Caillaud, Fadila	ERL	FY13	65.00	35.50	35.50
Health, Nutrition, and Population										
P074212	Health Sector Reform Project—Second Phase	Subcomp 1.B: Support for National Programs for mothers and children	IBRD/IDA	Bolivia	Bortman, Carlos Marcelo	APL	FY01	70.00	9.83	12.54

table continues next page

B. Components of Operations (continued)

Project ID	Project name	Component name	Product line	Country	TTL	Lending instrument	Approval date	Total project cost	Total invested on ECD (in US$ million, nominal)	Total invested on ECD (in US$ million, US$ of 2013)
P071062	Health Sector Development Project	Comp 1: Improve Health Services) physical and human capacity of health facilities, safe-motherhood programs, integrated management of childhood illnesses), malaria control, immunization)	IBRD/IDA	Djibouti	Ali, Sami	APL	FY02	30.00	5.00	6.27
P043254	Health Reform Support Project (HRSP)	Subcomp 1.2: Provision of a package of integrated maternal and child health services	IBRD/IDA	Yemen, Rep.	Al-Ahmadi, Afrah Alawi	SIL	FY02	29.60	18.17	22.79
P078324	Health Sector Emergency Reconstruction and Development Project	Comp 1. Expand the delivery of the basic package of health services (infant and child mortality, maternal mortality, child malnutrition)[en]million)	IBRD/IDA	Afghanistan	Capobianco, Emanuele	ERL	FY03	59.60	46.50	57.30
P076802	DO: Health Reform Support (APL)	Comp. 1—Health Services Coverage Extension (Maternal and child health)	IBRD/IDA	Dominican Republic	Montenegro Torres, Fernando	APL	FY03	42.71	17.70	21.81
P070542	Health Sector Support Project	Subcomp 2.2—Nutrition Programs (under Improved programs addressing public health priorities)	IBRD/IDA	Cambodia	Ly, Nareth	SIML	FY03	31.84	2.00	2.46

table continues next page

B. Components of Operations (continued)

Project ID	Project name	Component name	Product line	Country	TTL	Lending instrument	Approval date	Total project cost	Total invested on ECD (in US$ million, nominal)	Total invested on ECD (in US$ million, US$ of 2013)
P076715	Grenada: HIV/AIDS Prevention and Control	Subcomp 2f: Prevention of HIV/AIDS Mother-to-Child Transmission	IBRD/IDA	Grenada	Chao, Shiyan	APL	FY03	7.22	0.22	0.28
P050740	Sri Lanka: Health Sector Development	Subcomp 2.1: Family Health Program and Nutrition/ Subcomponent 2.2: immunization	IBRD/IDA	Sri Lanka	Navaratne, Kumari Vinodhani	SIL	FY04	72.60	5.00	6.02
P071025	AR-Provincial Maternal-Child Health Investment Project (1st. phase APL)	Comp 1: Implementation of maternal-child health insurance program	IBRD/IDA	Argentina	Cortez, Rafael A.	APL	FY04	289.90	112.10	135.08
P078971	Health Sector Reform 2 Project (APL #2)	Comp 1: maternity and neonatal care	IBRD/IDA	Romania	Florescu, Richard	APL	FY05	206.49	21.18	24.77
P088751	DRC Health Sector Rehabilitation Support Project	Comp 1: Expand Access and Utilization of a Proven Package of Essential Health Services to Selected Districts and Health Zones: Child preventative health interventions, reproductive and neonatal health services, integrated management of childhood illnesses; community-level activities	IBRD/IDA	Congo, Dem. Rep.	Frere, Jean-Jacques	SIL	FY06	150.00	104.00	117.73

table continues next page

B. Components of Operations *(continued)*

Project ID	Project name	Component name	Product line	Country	TTL	Lending instrument	Approval date	Total project cost	Total invested on ECD (in US$ million, nominal)	Total invested on ECD (in US$ million, US$ of 2013)
P098358	Afghanistan Health (supplement)	Comp 1. Expand the delivery of the basic package of health services (infant and child mortality, maternal mortality, child malnutrition)	IBRD/IDA	Afghanistan	Loevinsohn, Benjamin P.	ERL	FY06	30.00	16.10	18.23
P100966	Second Community Nutrition-Additional Financing	Comp 1: Community Nutrition Program	IBRD/IDA	Madagascar	Qamruddin, Jumana N.	SIL	FY07	15.00	5.00	5.50
P097181	Nutrition Enhancement Program II	Comp 1—Community-based nutrition	IBRD/IDA	Senegal	Mulder-Sibanda, Menno	APL	FY07	42.40	10.40	11.44
P095515	AR Provincial Maternal-Child Health Investment APL 2	Comp 1—Implementation of the Maternal-Child Health Insurance program	IBRD/IDA	Argentina	Cortez, Rafael A.	APL	FY07	646.30	242.70	267.08
P112142	Health and SP Project	Comp 1: Protecting Health and Nutritional Status	IBRD/IDA	Kyrgyz Republic	Rabie, Tamer Samah	ERL	FY08	6.00	1.00	1.08
P110658	Afghanistan Health (supplement II)	Comp1. Expand the delivery of the basic package of health services (infant and child mortality, maternal mortality, child malnutrition)	IBRD/IDA	Afghanistan	Capobianco, Emanuele	ERL	FY08	20.00	16.60	17.88

table continues next page

B. Components of Operations (continued)

Project ID	Project name	Component name	Product line	Country	TTL	Lending instrument	Approval date	Total project cost	Total invested on ECD (in US$ million, nominal)	Total invested on ECD (in US$ million, US$ of 2013)
P106228	Ethiopia Nutrition (FY08)	Comp 1: Supporting Service Delivery: Community-Based Nutrition (CBN) and Micronutrient Interventions	IBRD/IDA	Ethiopia	Hyder, Ziauddin	SIL	FY08	39.60	16.00	17.24
P101206	Expanding Access to Reduce Health Inequities Project (APL III)—Former Health Sector Reform—Third Phase (APL III)	Comp 2: Family, Community and Intercultural Health: improve access to maternal and infant health services	IBRD/IDA	Bolivia	Gordillo-Tobar, Amparo Elena	APL	FY08	26.20	9.90	10.66
P104527	Reproductive Health Vouchers in Western Uganda	Comp B: Safe child birth deliveries—antenatal, postnatal,	REA	Uganda	Okwero, Peter	SIL	FY08	4.30	2.15	2.32
P112446	Afghanistan—Strengthening Health Activities for the Rural Poor (SHARP)	Comp 1: Sustaining and strengthening the Basic Package of health Services (BPHS)	IBRD/IDA	Afghanistan	Haq, Inaam	SIL	FY09	126.00	19.00	20.14
P107395	Improving Health Sector Performance	Comp. 1—Improving the Health Service Delivery performance	IBRD/IDA	Djibouti	Ali, Sami	APL	FY09	8.00	3.60	3.82

table continues next page

B. Components of Operations *(continued)*

Project ID	Project name	Component name	Product line	Country	TTL	Lending instrument	Approval date	Total project cost	Total invested on ECD (in US$ million, nominal)	Total invested on ECD (in US$ million, US$ of 2013)
P106445	Health Equity and Performance Improvement Project	Comp 1: Ensuring access to primary health care services by the poor in rural areas	IBRD/IDA	Panama	Bonilla-Chacin, Maria Eugenia	SIL	FY09	58.73	25.80	27.34
P120669	Strengthening Health Activity For The Rural Poor Project	Comp 1: Sustaining and strengthening the Basic Package of health Services (BPHS)	IBRD/IDA	Afghanistan	Haq, Inaam	SIL	FY10	144.80	9.80	10.33
P115563	Uganda Health Systems Strengthening Project	Comp 4: Improved maternal, newborn and family planning services	IBRD/IDA	Uganda	Okwero, Peter	SIL	FY10	144.30	30.00	31.63
P117417	Nepal: Second HNP and HIV/AIDS Project	Improving the nutritional status of children and pregnant women (part of Comp 1: Health Service Delivery)	IBRD/IDA	Nepal	Belay, Tekabe Ayalew	SIML	FY10	129.15	12.92	13.62
P125677	DRC Polio Control Additional Financing to Health Sector Rehab Support	Comp 1: Expand Health Access and Utilization of a Proven Package of EHS to Selected Districts and Health Zones: integrated management of childhood diseases; maternal interventions including emergency obstetrical assistance and family planning services	IBRD/IDA	Congo, Dem. Rep.	Frere, Jean-Jacques	ERL	FY11	30.00	27.00	27.97

table continues next page

B. Components of Operations *(continued)*

Project ID	Project name	Component name	Product line	Country	TTL	Lending instrument	Approval date	Total project cost	Total invested on ECD (in US$ million, nominal)	Total invested on ECD (in US$ million, US$ of 2013)
P125470	Additional Financing 2 Kyrgyz Health and SP	Comp. 3: Protecting Health and Nutritional Status	IBRD/IDA	Kyrgyz Republic	Jaganjac, Nedim	SIL	FY11	24.00	2.60	2.69
P124906	Health Services Improvement Project (AF)	Subcomp—Free child (under 5) health services and equipment to support delivery of MCH services (Under Comp 1: Improving Quality and Utilization of Health Services)	IBRD/IDA	Lao PDR	Chanthala, Phetdara	SIL	FY11	12.40	5.03	5.21
P118708	Bangladesh—Health Sector Development Program	Subcomp 1.a: Improving Health Programs (Under Comp 1: Improving Health Services)	IBRD/IDA	Bangladesh	El-Saharty, Sameh	SIL	FY11	8011.00	22.84	23.66
P095171	Integrated Health and Water Management Project (SWAP)	Comp 1: Contribute to reducing the IMR (neonatal and postneonatal) in the State of Bahia.	IBRD/IDA	Brazil	Lavadenz, Fernando	SIL	FY11	60.00	48.59	50.32
P120349	BZ JSDF Improving Children's Health	Comp 1: Prevent and address malnutrition in children under 5 by empowering local community	REA	Belize	Carpio, Carmen	TAL	FY11	3.00	0.17	0.18

table continues next page

B. Components of Operations (continued)

Project ID	Project name	Component name	Product line	Country	TTL	Lending instrument	Approval date	Total project cost	Total invested on ECD (in US$ million, nominal)	Total invested on ECD (in US$ million, US$ of 2013)
P128169	Second Multi-sectoral STI/HIV/AIDS Prev II Additional Financing Project	Subcomponents 1,2,3: Integrated package for pregnant women at facility level, integrated package for children under 5 at facility level, support to health and nutrition services and community level	IBRD/IDA	Madagascar	Qamruddin, Jumana N.	SIL	FY12	6.00	2.90	2.95
P126088	DRC Additional Financing Primary Health Care	Component 1: expand access and utilization of a proven package of essential health services to selected districts and health zones	IBRD/IDA	Congo, Dem. Rep.	Frere, Jean-Jacques	SIL	FY13	75.00	62.50	62.50
P118806	Sri Lanka—Second Health Sector Development Project	Comp 1—thematic area 1—addressing maternal and child health and nutrition	IBRD/IDA	Sri Lanka	Navaratne, Kumari Vinodhani	SIML	FY13	200.00	63.30	63.30
P123394	Punjab Health Sector Reform Project	Sub-components 1 and 2: Integrated Management of maternal Neonatal and Child Health and Lady Health Workers; Introduction of Nutrition Services	IBRD/IDA	Pakistan	Haq, Inaam Ul	IPF	FY13	100.00	18.89	18.89

table continues next page

B. Components of Operations *(continued)*

Project ID	Project name	Component name	Product line	Country	TTL	Lending instrument	Approval date	Total project cost	Total invested on ECD (in US$ million, nominal)	Total invested on ECD (in US$ million, US$ of 2013)
P131194	DJ Improving Health Sector Performance	Subcomponents 1a, 1b, 1c, 1d: maternal and neonatal health services, integrated management of childhood illnesses, nutrition services, expanded program on immunization	IBRD/IDA	Djibouti	Ali, Sami	SIL	FY13	7.00	4.00	4.00
P120435	Kyrgyz Health Results-Based Financing	Component 1: Pilot Performance-Based Payments and Enhanced Supervision for Quality of Care maternal and neonatal care	REA	Kyrgyz Republic	Sargaldakova, Asel	SIL	FY13	0.00	9.59	9.59
Social Protection										
P069964	Human Capital Protection	Comp 2: Health/Nutrition Grant	IBRD/IDA	Colombia	Vermehren, Andrea	SIL	FY01	455.00	74.10	94.60
P081511	Supplemental Grant—Second Social Action Project		IBRD/IDA	Burundi	Kantabaze, Pamphile	SIL	FY03	14.90	3.00	3.70
P088857	CO TAL to support the 2nd PSAL	Subcomp 2D: Improve Coverage and efficiency of preschool ED (5-year-old children)	IBRD/IDA	Colombia	Coudouel, Aline	SIL	FY05	2.00	0.40	0.47
P082242	Nutrition and SP project	Comp 2: Consolidation and Expansion of the AIN-C program	IBRD/IDA	Honduras	McEvoy, Karla J.	SIL	FY06	23.30	12.00	13.58

table continues next page

B. Components of Operations *(continued)*

Project ID	Project name	Component name	Product line	Country	TTL	Lending instrument	Approval date	Total project cost	Total invested on ECD (in US$ million, nominal)	Total invested on ECD (in US$ million, US$ of 2013)
P093096	SOCIAL INCLUSION PROJECT	Comp 2: Inclusive Early Childhood ED Program	IBRD/IDA	Romania	Florescu, Richard	SIL	FY06	74.40	7.56	8.56
P101084	BO: Investing in Children and Youth	Comp 1—Implementing and scaling up the SP Program for Mothers and Children to combat chronic malnutrition	IBRD/IDA	Bolivia	Blanco, Gaston Mariano	SIL	FY08	19.55	12.40	13.36
P098328	SP Project	Comp 3-Strenghening the supply of growth and development promotion interventions and securing access to health services for the RO program beneficiaries in indigenous areas	IBRD/IDA	Panama	Blanco, Gaston Mariano	SIL	FY08	46.94	10.00	10.77
P114441	Price Vulnerability (Food Crisis) /former Product ID: P113225	Sub component of Component 1: Support Integral School Nutrition Program (both preprimary and primary)	SF (bank executed)	Nicaragua	Montenegro Lazo, Miriam Matilde	ERL	FY09	8.00	1.08	1.14
P121779	Nicaragua SP	promote preschool (and primary school) attendance through provision of school lunches	IBRD/IDA	Nicaragua	Jones, Theresa	SIL	FY11	19.50	2.25	2.33
P126339	Egypt Emergency Labor Intensive Investment Project	Sub projects: Early childhood education services and rehabilitation of kindergartens	IBRD/IDA	Egypt, Arab Rep.	Al-Ahmadi, Afrah Alawi	ERL	FY12	200.00	2.50	2.54

table continues next page

B. Components of Operations (continued)

Project ID	Project name	Component name	Product line	Country	TTL	Lending instrument	Approval date	Total project cost	Total invested on ECD (in US$ million, nominal)	Total invested on ECD (in US$ million, US$ of 2013)
P127200	TOGO Community Development and Safety Nets Project	Subcomponent 2.2—pilot cash transfers in regions with high malnutrition	IBRD/IDA	Togo	Van Dyck, John	SIL	FY12	14.00	2.00	2.03
P130328	DJ Crisis Response—Social Safety Net Project	Component 2: nutrition-based social assistance to support investments in human capital	IBRD/IDA	Djibouti	Koettl—Brodmann, Stefanie	ERL	FY12	5.00	1.22	1.24
P125610	Nepal: School Sector Reform Program Additional Financing	Sub-component 1.3: Early Childhood Education and Development—expand ECED services for children of four years of age to prepare them for basic education	IBRD/IDA	Nepal	Al-Ahmadi, Afrah Alawi	SIL	FY13	100.00	16.00	16.00
P127328	Emergency Safety Nets project (Jigiséméjiri)	Sub-component 1C: Pilot Preventive Nutrition Package to children under five years old and pregnant women	IBRD/IDA	Mali	Auffret, Philippe	ERL	FY13	70.00	3.70	3.70

Note: APL = Adaptable Program Loan; DPL = Development Policy Loan; ECD = early childhood development; ECED = early childhood education and development; ERL = Emergency Recovery Loan; FY = fiscal year; IBRD = International Bank for Reconstruction and Development; IDA = International Development Association; IPF = Investment Project Financing; LIL = Learning and Innovation Loan; P4R = Program for Results; REA = Recipient Executed Activity; SF = Social Fund; SIL = Specific Investment Loan; SIML = Sector Investment and Maintenance Loan; TAL = Technical Assistance Loan; TTL = Task Team Leader.

B.2 Analytical Activities (Economic and Sector Work, Technical Assistance, Impact Evaluations, Knowledge Products, Global Partnership Programs, and Programmatic Approaches)

Project ID	Project name	Product line	Country/Region	TTL	Approval date	Total invested on ECD (in US$ million, nominal)	Total invested on ECD (in US$ million, US$ of 2013)
Education							
TF024055	BNPP-EDUC/CULT/DEV: BREAKING THE POVERTY CYCLE (EARLY CHILDHOOD DEVELOPMENT)	TA	World	Mary Eming Young	FY01	0.39	0.49
P072053	Egypt Early Childhood Development	ESW	Egypt, Arab Rep.	Chang, Mae Chu	FY02	0.62	0.78
P077850	Early Childhood Development in Africa: Can We Do More for Less? A Look at Impact and Implications of Preschools in Cape Verde & Guinea	ESW	Africa	Jaramillo, Adriana	FY02	0.00	0.00
TF050206	BNPP-CAPACITY/BUILD:TRAINING AND CAPACITY BUILD-ING ON ECD IN THE MIDDLE EAST AND NORTH AFRICA REGION	TA	Middle East and North Africa	Arun R. Joshi	FY02	0.36	0.45
TF041006	ERITREA—INTEGRATED EARLY CHILDHOOD DEVELOPMENT PROGRAM—SECTOR WORK	ESW	Eritrea	Christine Lao Pena	FY02	0.02	0.02
P080624	Egypt Early Childhood ED Policy Dialogue	ESW	Egypt, Arab Rep.	Chang, Mae Chu	FY03	0.01	0.01
P075882	Support to Jordan Early Childhood Development	TA	Jordan	Chang, Mae Chu	FY03	0.09	0.12
P087089	Early Childhood Development	ESW	ECA	Schweitzer, Eluned	FY04	0.06	0.07
P092267	Early Child Development Capacity-Building Initiative	GPP	World	Young, Mary Eming	FY04	8.00	9.64
P076188	Regional ECD Capacity Building Program	TA	Middle East and North Africa	Joshi, Arun R.	FY05	0.39	0.46
TF055298	CREATION OF ECD RESOURCE MATERIAL	TA	World	Keith Mackay	FY05	0.01	0.02
TF054403	IDF-UNESCO:GRANT AGREEMENT FOR STRENGTHENING NA-TIONAL HIV/AIDS RESPONSES TO THE NEEDS OF YOUNG CHILDREN IN PARTICIPATING STATES OF	TA	Africa	Young, Mary Eming	FY05	0.30	0.35

table continues next page

B.2 Analytical Activities (Economic and Sector Work, Technical Assistance, Impact Evaluations, Knowledge Products, Global Partnership Programs, and Programmatic Approaches) *(continued)*

Project ID	Project name	Product line	Country/Region	TTL	Approval date	Total invested on ECD (in US$ million, nominal)	Total invested on ECD (in US$ million, US$ of 2013)
P093916	ID-ECED Situation Analysis	ESW	Indonesia	Chang, Mae Chu	FY06	0.05	0.05
TF056416	BNPP-BASIC EDUC: PROMOTING LEADERSHIP AND CAPACITY FOR EARLY CHILDHOOD DEV. IN AFRICA	TA	Africa	Mary Eming Young	FY06	0.50	0.57
TF056580	PHRD–JAMAICA: EARLY CHILDHOOD DEVELOPMENT	TA	Jamaica	Christoph Kurowski	FY06	0.51	0.58
P099767	MP Pilot on Integrated Child Develop. IE (P099767) (removed P097663) IE-P099767-IMPE-TF096294	ESW	India	Sankar, Deepa	FY06	0.15	0.16
TF058249	PROGRAMMATIC SUPPORT TO IEG'S ECD ACTIVITIES	TA	World	Nidhi Khattri	FY07	0.04	0.04
P103081	Early Childhood Development in Latin America and the Caribbean	ESW	Latin America and the Caribbean	Vegas, Emiliana	FY08	0.18	0.20
P105133	Monitoring Outcome for School Readiness	GPP	World	Young, Mary Eming	FY08	0.00	0.00
TF091016	THE GAMBIA—COMMUNITY-BASED EARLY CHILDHOOD CARE AND DEVELOPMENT (ECD)	TA	Gambia	Yi-Kyoung Lee	FY08	0.04	0.04
TF092053	EARLY CHILDHOOD CARE AND DEVELOPMENT—NUTRITION	TA	Africa	Marito Garcia	FY08	3.38	3.65
TF091145	SIEF—RIO DE JANEIRO RANDOMIZED EVALUATION OF INTEGRATED ECD PROGRAM	TA	Brazil	Pedro Olinto	FY08	0.12	0.13
P111691	Africa ECD Regional Programme	TA	Africa	Devercelli, Amanda Epstein	FY08	4.40	4.74
P090645	Early Childhood Care and Development	TA	Vietnam	Vu, Binh Thanh	FY08	0.01	0.01
P110517	ID—ECD Evaluation Study	IE	Indonesia	Hasan, Amer	FY08	0.00	0.00
P100396	hdnvp/CE-Promoting ECD and School Readiness	ESW	World		FY09	0.02	0.02

table continues next page

B.2 Analytical Activities (Economic and Sector Work, Technical Assistance, Impact Evaluations, Knowledge Products, Global Partnership Programs, and Programmatic Approaches) *(continued)*

Project ID	Project name	Product line	Country/Region	TTL	Approval date	Total invested on ECD (in US$ million, nominal)	Total invested on ECD (in US$ million, US$ of 2013)
P115569	BR Early Childhood Development Conference	TA	Brazil	Evans, David-	FY09	0.14	0.15
TF094095	NIGERIA—EARLY CHILDHOOD CARE AND DEVELOPMENT	TA	Nigeria	Olatunde Adetoyese Adekola	FY09	0.12	0.13
TF094525	ZAMBIA—EARLY CHILDHOOD CARE AND DEVELOPMENT	TA	Zambia	Carla Bertoncino	FY09	0.11	0.12
TF094550	LIBERIA—EARLY CHILDHOOD CARE AND DEVELOPMENT	TA	Liberia	Keiko Inoue	FY09	0.06	0.07
TF094397	GUINEA—EARLY CHILDHOOD CARE AND DEVELOPMENT PROGRAM	TA	Guinea	Nathalie Lahire	FY09	0.09	0.10
P113999	KH-Early Childhood ED IE	IE	Cambodia	Filmer, Deon P.	FY09	0.44	0.46
P116849	CL (FBS) ECD Institutions	ESW	Chile	Bruns, Barbara	FY10	0.07	0.07
P118411	ECD For Regional Centers	GPP	World		FY10	0.24	0.26
P111566	FFS Preschool and ECD Khanty-Mansiysk AO	TA	Russia	Froumin, Isak	FY10	0.20	0.21
P117850	Improvement of the Regional Early Childhood Development and Preschool ED System	TA	Russia	Froumin, Isak	FY10	0.01	0.01
P116857	Early Childhood Care and Development Initiative (EPDF funding)	TA	Zambia	Bertoncino, Carla	FY10	0.11	0.12
TF096544	IE of ECD in Mozambique	TA	Mozambique	Sophie Naudeau	FY10	0.14	0.15
P119415	Regional Early Childhood Development Studies	ESW	Middle East and North Africa	Wright, Christina D.	FY11	0.20	0.21
P113762	CN-Early Childhood Development	ESW	China	Wu, Kin Bing	FY11	0.18	0.18
P117588	BR Early Childhood	ESW	Brazil	Evans, David-000213993	FY11	0.25	0.25

table continues next page

TABLE B.2 Analytical Activities (Economic and Sector Work, Technical Assistance, Impact Evaluations, Knowledge Products, Global Partnership Programs, and Programmatic Approaches) *(continued)*

Project ID	Project name	Product line	Country/Region	TTL	Approval date	Total invested on ECD (in US$ million, nominal)	Total invested on ECD (in US$ million, US$ of 2013)
P122358	ECD and Poverty	ESW	World	Sophie Naudeau	FY11	0.00	0.00
TF098115	Tanzania—Early Childhood Care and Development (ECD)	TA	Tanzania	Arun R. Joshi	FY11	0.14	0.14
TF097794	Middle East and North Africa Early Childhood Development (ECD) Country Studies	TA	Middle East and North Africa	Christina D. Wright	FY11	0.09	0.09
TF099262	Brazil Knowledge Platform for Early Child Development Monitoring and Evaluation (ECD M&E)	TA	Brazil	David Evans	FY11	0.05	0.05
TF099715	Improved ECD Policies in Honduras and Nicaragua	TA	Latin America and the Caribbean	Peter Anthony Holland	FY11	0.09	0.09
P125083	FBS-08-FY11: TA to prepare a concept for preschool ED development	TA	Russia	Shmis, Tigran	FY11	0.15	0.16
P123497	BR Early Childhood Development NLTA	TA	Brazil	Evans, David	FY12	0.60	0.60
P130808	Investing in Early Childhood Development (ECD)	GPP	World	Wodon, Quentin	FY12	0.75	0.76
P123649	SABER ECD	KMP	World	Neuman, Michelle J.	FY12	0.09	0.09
P129586	Uzbekistan: Improving Early Childhood Care and Education	ESW	Uzbekistan	Naqvi, Naveed Hassan	FY13	0.75	0.75
P132355	MZ—Impact Evaluation of Scaled-up Early Childhood Development Activities	IE	Mozambique	Naudeau, Sophie	FY13	0.60	0.60
P132719	Early Childhood Development TA	TA	Russia	Shmis, Tigran	FY13	0.15	0.15
P132905	Middle East and North Africa Early Childhood Development Support	TA	Middle East and North Africa	El-Kogali, Safaa El Tayeb	FY13	0.10	0.10
P133742	Early Childhood Care and Education	ESW	Sri Lanka	Bhatta, Saurav Dev	FY13	0.19	0.19

table continues next page

TABLE B.2 Analytical Activities (Economic and Sector Work, Technical Assistance, Impact Evaluations, Knowledge Products, Global Partnership Programs, and Programmatic Approaches) *(continued)*

Project ID	Project name	Product line	Country/Region	TTL	Approval date	Total invested on ECD (in US$ million, nominal)	Total invested on ECD (in US$ million, US$ of 2013)
P143076	Evaluating closing gap between Roma and non-Roma in Bulgaria through preschool participation: outreach and conditional food coupons	IE	Bulgaria	de Laat, Joost	FY13	0.70	0.70
P144511	The medium-term effects of a home-based early childhood development intervention in Colombia	IE	Colombia	Galasso, Emanuela	FY13	0.54	0.54
P145066	Indonesia Early Childhood Education and Development Programmatic AAA	PA	Indonesia	Hasan, Amer	FY13	0.65	0.65
P145155	Early Childhood Care and Education	TA	India	Arif, Umbreen	FY13	0.20	0.20
P109237	ECD and ECE Policy	KMP	Multi-Regional	Wodon, Quentin	FY13	0.40	0.40
P131755	Middle East and North Africa Regional Work on ECD	TA	Middle East and North Africa	El-Kogali, Safaa El Tayeb	FY13	0.09	0.09
P132048	ECD Framework for HD Sector	KMP	World	Wodon, Quentin	FY13	0.10	0.10
P143085	Malawi ECD Impact Evaluation	IE	Malawi	Wodon, Quentin	FY13	0.95	0.95
P144229	RAS on ECD system development for Khanty-Mansiysk region	TA	Russia	Shmis, Tigran	FY13	0.03	0.03
P144137	Africa Early Learning Partnership	PA	Africa	Devercelli, Amanda Epstein	FY13	0.00	0.00
P129208	China Early Child Development	TA	China	Liang, Xiaoyan	FY13	0.33	0.33
P144498	ELP—Regional Activities	ESW	Africa	Devercelli, Amanda Epstein	FY13	0.10	0.10
P144501	ELP—Country Activities	ESW	Africa	Devercelli, Amanda Epstein	FY13	0.13	0.13

table continues next page

B.2 Analytical Activities (Economic and Sector Work, Technical Assistance, Impact Evaluations, Knowledge Products, Global Partnership Programs, and Programmatic Approaches) *(continued)*

Project ID	Project name	Product line	Country/Region	TTL	Approval date	Total invested on ECD (in US$ million, nominal)	Total invested on ECD (in US$ million, US$ of 2013)
Health, Nutrition, and Population							
P073541	National Nutrition Action Plan for Yemen	ESW	Yemen, Rep.	Abdel-Hamid, Alaa Mahmoud Hamed	FY02	0.04	0.05
P081233	Maternal and Child Health: Reaching the Poor	ESW	World	Wagstaff, Adam	FY04	0.00	0.00
P094568	Repositioning Nutrition in the Bank	ESW	World	Shekar, Meera	FY05	0.39	0.46
P084976	Impact Evaluation of Selected Nutrition Projects in India	ESW	India	Gragnolati, Michele	FY05	0.31	0.37
P095541	EC-Nutrition Review	ESW	Ecuador	Walker, David Ian	FY06	0.21	0.24
P098336	Tanzania Nutrition Study	ESW	Tanzania	Hoogeveen, Johannes G.	FY07	0.12	0.13
TF058188	FAMILY SIZE AND INVESTMENTS IN EARLY CHILDHOOD DEVELOPMENTS	TA	Ecuador	Norbert R. Schady	FY07	0.11	0.12
P099662	Malnutrition in Sri Lanka	ESW	Sri Lanka	Shekar, Meera	FY08	0.12	0.13
P111025	Building Operational Capacities for Scaling-Up Nutrition	GPP	World	Shekar, Meera	FY08	0.01	0.01
P113822	Scaling-Up Nutrition Investments	GPP	World	Elder, Leslie K.	FY09	1.34	1.42
P115881	Regional: Expanding Regional Response to Malnutrition	TA	South Asia	Mbuya, Nkosinathi Vusizihlobo	FY09	1.50	1.59
P107544	Infant and Child Feeding Study	ESW	Malawi	Dutta, Sheila	FY10	0.13	0.14
P121309	Bridging the Knowledge Gap for Results in Maternal, Newborn, Child Health	GPP	World	Al Tuwaijri, Sameera Maziad	FY10	1.20	1.27
TF097107	IE of 3 types of ECD interventions in Cambodia (SIEF)	TA	Cambodia	Sophie Naudeau	FY10	0.20	0.21

table continues next page

TABLE B.2 Analytical Activities (Economic and Sector Work, Technical Assistance, Impact Evaluations, Knowledge Products, Global Partnership Programs, and Programmatic Approaches) *(continued)*

Project ID	Project name	Product line	Country/Region	TTL	Approval date	Total invested on ECD (in US$ million, nominal)	Total invested on ECD (in US$ million, US$ of 2013)
P117060	Rwanda Health system strengthening—HRBF pilot activities impact evaluation	ESW	Rwanda	Workie, Netsanet Walelign	FY10	1.66	1.75
P123319	Bridging the Knowledge Gap for Results in Maternal, New-born, Child Health	GPP	World	Al Tuwaijri, Sameera Maziad	FY11	0.34	0.35
P106706	Community-Based Health and Nutrition Study	ESW	Nigeria	Cisse, Boubou	FY11	0.43	0.44
P113434	Bangladesh—Multisectoral Nutrition Part II	ESW	Bangladesh	Mbuya, Nkosinathi Vusizihlobo	FY11	0.05	0.05
P130715	BHUTAN NATIONAL NUTRITION ASSESSMENT AND GAP ANALYSIS	ESW	Bhutan	Nagpal, Somil	FY12	0.11	0.11
P115126	Argentina—HRITF Impact Evaluation—maternal-child provincial investment	IE	Argentina	Vermeersch, Christel M. J.	Fy12	0.78	0.79
P131471	Healthy Mothers and Babies:	IE	Nigeria	Di Maro, Vincenzo	FY12	0.20	0.20
P129207	Central African Republic Impact Evaluation of Result-Based Financing in the Health Sector	IE	Central African Republic	Sorgho, Gaston	FY12	1.50	1.52
P124466	RSR MDTF—Improving Latin America and the Caribbean country responses to protect the nutritional status of the poorest and most vulnerable in times of crises	KMP	Latin America	Carpio, Carmen	FY12	0.26	0.26
P143293	Addressing Malnutrition in Madagascar—PNNC/Seecaline	IE	Madagascar	Qamruddin, Jumana N.	FY13	0.50	0.50
P144188	Piloting the nutrition/workfare SSN	IE	Djibouti	Koettl—Brodmann, Stefanie	FY13	0.51	0.51
P145415	Long-Term Effects of Nutrition at Birth	IE	Indonesia	Giles, John T.	FY13	2.49	2.49
P132759	Building parental capacity to help child nutrition and health: a randomized controlled trial	IE	Bangladesh	Vawda, Ayesha Y.	FY13	0.74	0.74

table continues next page

B.2 Analytical Activities (Economic and Sector Work, Technical Assistance, Impact Evaluations, Knowledge Products, Global Partnership Programs, and Programmatic Approaches) *(continued)*

Project ID	Project name	Product line	Country/Region	TTL	Approval date	Total invested on ECD (in US$ million, nominal)	Total invested on ECD (in US$ million, US$ of 2013)
P143136	TA for GOI Community-based Health and Nutrition to Reduce Stunting Project	TA	Indonesia	Dorkin, Darren W.	FY13	0.93	0.93
P143173	Impact Evaluation: assess the impact of early childhood stimulation	IE	India	Govindaraj, Ramesh	FY13	0.68	0.68
P144126	Maternal and Child Health and Nutrition in Lao PDR: Evidence from a Household Survey in Six Central and Southern Provinces	ESW	Lao PDR	Tandon, Ajay	FY13	0.03	0.03
P145607	Strengthening the Government of Bangladesh's Response to Malnutrition	PA	Bangladesh	Mbuya, Nkosinathi Vusizihlobo	FY13	0.39	0.39
P129498	Protecting and Promoting Access to Maternal and Neonatal Health Services	TA	Tajikistan	Giuffrida, Antonino	FY13	0.40	0.40
P132126	Lesotho HRITF Impact Evaluation—maternal and newborn health performance based financing	IE	Lesotho	Yamashita-Allen, Kanako	FY13	1.50	1.50
P143433	Out-of-Pocket Expenditures on MCH	ESW	Lao PDR	Tandon, Ajay	FY13	0.03	0.03
P144441	Nigeria Saving One Million Lives Initiative	TA	Nigeria	Nair, Dinesh M.	FY13	0.16	0.16
Social Protection							
TF024242	BURUNDI SOCIAL ACTION PROGRAM-EARLY CHILDHOOD DEVELOPMENT COMPONENT	TA	Burundi	Pamphile Kantabaze	FY01	0.88	1.13
P111223	EC Child Development	TA	Ecuador	Marini, Alessandra	FY10	0.18	0.19
P119019	EC Child Development II	TA	Ecuador	Gutierrez, Nelson	FY11	0.10	0.10
P133583	Niger Safety Nets Project Impact Evaluation	IE	Niger	Premand, Patrick	FY13	0.98	0.98

Note: ECA = Europe and Central Asia; ECD = early childhood development; ESW = Economic and Sector Work; FY = fiscal year; GPP = Global Partnership Program; IE = Impact Evaluation; KMP = Knowledge Product; PA = Poverty Assessment; TA = Task Team Leader; TTL = Technical Assistance.

B.3 Projects Likely to Benefit Young Children (Lending and Trust Funded)

Project ID	Project name	Product line	Country	TTL	Lending instrument	Approval year	Total lending amount (US$, nominal)	Total lending amount, US$ (2013)
Education								
P044803	PRIMARY EDUCATION FOR DISADVANTAGED CHILDREN PROJECT	IBRD/IDA	Vietnam	Vu, Binh Thanh	SIL	FY03	138.76	170.98
P077757	CUNDINAMARCA EDUCATION QUALITY IMPROVEMENT	IBRD/IDA	Colombia	Laverde, Martha	SIL	FY03	15.00	18.48
P080746	HD PRGM. SECTOR REFORM LOAN	IBRD/IDA	Brazil	Lindert, Kathy A.	SAL	FY03	505.05	622.34
P055459	ELEMENTARY EDUCATION PROJECT	IBRD/IDA	India	Kaul, Venita	SIL	FY04	500.00	602.48
P070963	Argentina Rural Education Improvement Project—PROMER	IBRD/IDA	Argentina	Holland, Peter Anthony	SIL	FY06	150.00	169.80
P077903	Third Education Project—Phase II	IBRD/IDA	Gambia	Lahire, Nathalie	APL	FY06	8.00	9.06
P088728	Mexico Education Quality	IBRD/IDA	Mexico	Silveira, Ricardo Rocha	APL	FY06	240.00	271.69
P086875	Education and Training Sector Improvement Program—ETSIP	IBRD/IDA	Namibia	Vodopivec, Milan	DPL	FY07	7.50	8.25
P094042	BASIC EDUCATION, Phase I	IBRD/IDA	Uzbekistan	Latif, Scherezad Joya Monami	APL	FY07	15.00	16.51
P101243	Punjab Education Development Policy Credit—IV	IBRD/IDA	Pakistan	Khan, Tahseen Sayed	DPL	FY07	100.00	110.05
P082908	Colombia Rural Education Project (APL Phase II)	IBRD/IDA	Colombia	Laverde, Martha	APL	FY08	40.00	43.09

table continues next page

B.3 Projects Likely to Benefit Young Children (Lending and Trust Funded) *(continued)*

Project ID	Project name	Product line	Country	TTL	Lending instrument	Approval year	Total lending amount (US$, nominal)	Total lending amount, US$ (2013)
P110642	Basic Education Sector Project—Additional Financing	IBRD/IDA	Burkina Faso	Ouedraogo, Adama	SIL	FY08	15.00	16.16
P112321	Central African Republic: EFA-FTI Catalytic Fund Preparation	REA	Central African Republic	Dung-Kim Pham	SIL	FY09	37.80	40.06
P107845	Second Basic Education	IBRD/IDA	Uzbekistan	Naqvi, Naveed Hassan	APL	FY10	28.00	29.52
P125127	MZ-Education Sector Support Program	IBRD/IDA	Mozambique	Naudeau, Sophie	SIL	FY11	71.00	73.54
P111661	Tertiary Education Finance for Results Project III	IBRD/IDA	Chile	Sundararaman, Venkatesh	SIL	FY12	40.00	40.66
P130853	Yemen, Rep.: Second Basic Education Development Project	IBRD/IDA	Yemen, Rep.	Wang, Lianqin	SIL	FY13	66.00	66.00
P133333	Senegal Quality and Equity of Basic Education	IBRD/IDA	Senegal	Seck, Atou	SIL	FY13	20.00	20.00
P126408	Support to Uruguayan Public Schools Project	IBRD/IDA	Uruguay	Ambasz, Diego	SIL	FY13	40.00	40.00
P129381	Ghana Partnership for Education	REA	Ghana	Mikesell, Deborah Newitter	SIL	FY13	75.50	75.50
P128644	Sudan Basic Education Recovery Project	REA	Sudan	Fasih, Tazeen	ERL	FY13	76.50	76.50

table continues next page

B.3 Projects Likely to Benefit Young Children (Lending and Trust Funded) (continued)

Project ID	Project name	Product line	Country	TTL	Lending instrument	Approval year	Total lending amount (US$, nominal)	Total lending amount, US$ (2013)
Health, Nutrition, and Population								
P051174	Health Investment Fund Project	IBRD/IDA	Moldova	Jesse, Maris	SIL	FY01	10.00	12.77
P060329	HIV/AIDS Rapid Response Project	IBRD/IDA	Gambia	May, John F.	APL	FY01	15.00	19.15
P066321	Basic Health Care Project (03)	IBRD/IDA	Mexico	Macias, Claudia	SIL	FY01	350.00	446.82
P066486	Decentralized Reproductive Health and HIV/AIDS	IBRD/IDA	Kenya	Mills, Michael	SIL	FY01	50.00	63.83
P069886	Multisectoral HIV/AIDS Project	IBRD/IDA	Ethiopia	Okubagzhi, Gebreselassie	APL	FY01	59.70	76.21
P069933	HIV/AIDS Prevention Project	IBRD/IDA	Bangladesh	Nair, Dinesh M.	SIL	FY01	40.00	51.07
P070920	HIV/AIDS Disaster Response Project	IBRD/IDA	Kenya	Mills, Michael	APL	FY01	50.00	63.83
P071617	AIDS Response Project (GARFUND)	IBRD/IDA	Ghana	Diack, Aissatou	APL	FY01	25.00	31.92
P072482	HIV/AIDS Control Project	IBRD/IDA	Uganda	Okwero, Peter	APL	FY01	47.50	60.64
P073065	Multisectoral HIV/AIDS Project	IBRD/IDA	Cameroon	Mkouonga, Francois Honore	APL	FY01	50.00	63.83
P075220	CARIBBEAN HIV/AIDS I-BARBADOS	IBRD/IDA	Barbados	Godinho, Joana	APL	FY01	15.15	19.34
P053575	Health System Reform Project	IBRD/IDA	Honduras	Bortman, Carlos Marcelo	SIL	FY02	27.10	33.99
P057665	FAMILY HEALTH EXTENSION PROGRAM	IBRD/IDA	Brazil	La Forgia, Gerard Martin	APL	FY02	68.00	85.28

table continues next page

B.3 Projects Likely to Benefit Young Children (Lending and Trust Funded) (continued)

Project ID	Project name	Product line	Country	TTL	Lending instrument	Approval year	Total lending amount (US$, nominal)	Total lending amount, US$ (2013)
P067986	SV—Earthquake Emergency Recovery and Health Services Extension Project	IBRD/IDA	El Salvador	Cortez, Rafael A.	ERL	FY02	142.60	178.83
P069916	2nd Social Expenditure Management	IBRD/IDA	Philippines	Banzon, Eduardo P.	SIML	FY02	100.00	125.41
P070290	Second Health Systems Development	IBRD/IDA	Nigeria	Akala, Francisca Ayodeji	SIL	FY02	127.01	159.28
P070291	HIV/AIDS Program Development Project	IBRD/IDA	Nigeria	Akala, Francisca Ayodeji	APL	FY02	90.30	113.24
P071371	Multisectoral HIV/AIDS Control and Orphans Project	IBRD/IDA	Burundi	Kantabaze, Pamphile	APL	FY02	36.00	45.15
P071433	HIV/AIDS Disaster Response	IBRD/IDA	Burkina Faso	Subayi, Tshiya A.	APL	FY02	22.00	27.59
P071505	DO-HIV/AIDS Prevention and Control Proj.	IBRD/IDA	Dominican Republic	Montenegro Torres, Fernando	APL	FY02	25.00	31.35
P072226	Second Population and AIDS Project	IBRD/IDA	Chad	Cisse, Boubou	SIL	FY02	24.56	30.80
P073118	Multisectoral HIV/AIDS Project	IBRD/IDA	Benin	Ahouissoussi, Nicolas	APL	FY02	23.00	28.84
P073525	Multisectoral HIV/AIDS Project	IBRD/IDA	Central African Republic	Sorgho, Gaston	APL	FY02	17.00	21.32
P073883	HIV/AIDS Response Project	IBRD/IDA	Sierra Leone	Zampaglione, Giuseppe	APL	FY02	15.00	18.81
P074059	HIV/AIDS Prevention and Control Project	IBRD/IDA	Senegal	De St Antoine, Jean J.	APL	FY02	30.00	37.62

table continues next page

B.3 Projects Likely to Benefit Young Children (Lending and Trust Funded) *(continued)*

Project ID	Project name	Product line	Country	TTL	Lending instrument	Approval year	Total lending amount (US$, nominal)	Total lending amount, US$ (2013)
P074641	Second HIV/AIDS Project	IBRD/IDA	Jamaica	Chao, Shiyan	APL	FY02	15.00	18.81
P003248	Zambia National Response to HIV/AIDS (ZANARA)	IBRD/IDA	Zambia	Sunkutu, Musonda Rosemary	APL	FY03	42.00	51.75
P040555	Health Sector Development Project	IBRD/IDA	Georgia	Rokx, Claudia	SIL	FY03	20.30	25.01
P054119	Bahia Health System Reform Project	IBRD/IDA	Brazil	Lavadenz, Fernando	APL	FY03	30.00	36.97
P064237	Tuberculosis and AIDS Control Project	IBRD/IDA	Russia	Marquez, Patricio V.	SIL	FY03	150.00	184.83
P069857	Tuberculosis and HIV/AIDS Control Project	IBRD/IDA	Ukraine	Gracheva, Maria E.	SIL	FY03	60.00	73.93
P071374	Multi-Sectoral HIV/AIDS Project	IBRD/IDA	Rwanda	Schneidman, Miriam	APL	FY03	30.50	37.58
P071612	Multi-Sector STI/HIV/AIDS Support Project	IBRD/IDA	Niger	Johansen, Anne	SIL	FY03	25.00	30.81
P073378	Multisectoral AIDS Project (MAP)	IBRD/IDA	Guinea	Ousmane Diadie, Haidara	SIL	FY03	20.30	25.01
P073649	Second Health Sector Program Support Project	IBRD/IDA	Ghana	Rose, Laura L.	SIL	FY03	89.60	110.41
P073772	Health Workforce and Services (PHP 3)	IBRD/IDA	Indonesia	Marzoeki, Puti	SIL	FY03	105.60	130.12
P074122	AIDS CONTROL PROJECT	IBRD/IDA	Moldova	Eckertz, Dorothee B.	SIL	FY03	5.50	6.78
P074730	National HIV/AIDS Prevention Project	IBRD/IDA	Sri Lanka	Rosenhouse, Sandra	SIL	FY03	12.60	15.53

table continues next page

B.3 Projects Likely to Benefit Young Children (Lending and Trust Funded) *(continued)*

Project ID	Project name	Product line	Country	TTL	Lending instrument	Approval year	Total lending amount (US$, nominal)	Total lending amount, US$ (2013)
P075056	Food and Drugs Capacity Building Project	IBRD/IDA	India	Ramana, Gandham N.V.	SIL	FY03	54.03	66.58
P075528	Trinidad and Tobago: HIV/AIDS Prevention and Control Project	IBRD/IDA	Trinidad and Tobago	Chao, Shiyan	APL	FY03	20.00	24.64
P076798	KN: HIV/AIDS PREVENTION AND CONTROL PROJECT	IBRD/IDA	St. Kitts and Nevis	Chao, Shiyan	APL	FY03	4.05	4.99
P080295	Partnership for Polio Eradication Project	IBRD/IDA	Nigeria	Nair, Dinesh M.	SIL	FY03	28.70	35.37
P080400	AIDS and STD Control Project (03)	IBRD/IDA	Brazil	Godinho, Joana	SIL	FY03	100.00	123.22
P082395	Programmatic Human Development Reform Loan Project	IBRD/IDA	Ecuador	Dulitzky, Daniel	SAL	FY03	50.00	61.61
P071014	Multisectoral AIDS Project	IBRD/IDA	Tanzania	Haazen, Dominic S.	APL	FY04	70.00	84.35
P072637	Provincial Maternal-Child Health Sector Adjustment Ln. (PMCHSAL)	IBRD/IDA	Argentina	Gomez-Meza, Jose Pablo	SAL	FY04	750.00	903.72
P073442	HIV/AIDS GLOBAL MITIGATION SUPPORT PROJECT	IBRD/IDA	Guinea-Bissau	Prevoo, Dirk Nicolaas	SIL	FY04	7.00	8.43
P073821	Multisectoral AIDS Project (MAP)	IBRD/IDA	Malawi	Clark, John Paul	SIL	FY04	35.00	42.17
P073974	Health Systems Modernization Project	IBRD/IDA	Armenia	Hayrapetyan, Susanna	APL	FY04	19.00	22.89
P075979	Social Sector Support Project	IBRD/IDA	São Tomé and Príncipe	Martins, Geraldo Joao	SIL	FY04	6.50	7.83

table continues next page

B.3 Projects Likely to Benefit Young Children (Lending and Trust Funded) *(continued)*

Project ID	Project name	Product line	Country	TTL	Lending instrument	Approval year	Total lending amount (US$, nominal)	Total lending amount, US$ (2013)
P076722	HIV/AIDS PREVENTION and CONTROL PROJECT	IBRD/IDA	Guyana	Chao, Shiyan	APL	FY04	10.00	12.05
P077513	HIV/AIDS and Health (MAP program)	IBRD/IDA	Congo, Rep.	Louani, Mahamat Goadi	SIL	FY04	19.00	22.89
P078368	Multisector HIV/AIDS Control Project-ICR	IBRD/IDA	Mauritania	Subayi, Tshiya A.	SIL	FY04	21.00	25.30
P080721	THE PAN CARIBBEAN PARTNERSHIP AGAINST HIV/AIDS	IBRD/IDA	Latin American and the Caribbean	Chao, Shiyan	APL	FY04	9.00	10.84
P082335	Second Health Sector Development Project	IBRD/IDA	Tanzania	Haazen, Dominic S.	APL	FY04	65.00	78.32
P082516	DRC Multisectoral HIV/AIDS Project	IBRD/IDA	Congo, Dem. Rep.	Frere, Jean-Jacques	APL	FY04	102.00	122.91
P083013	VIGISUS APL 2—Disease Surveillance and Control	IBRD/IDA	Brazil	Godinho, Joana	APL	FY04	100.00	120.50
P040613	Nepal Health Sector Program Project	IBRD/IDA	Nepal	Voetberg, Albertus	SIML	FY05	50.00	58.48
P051370	Health 2 Project	IBRD/IDA	Uzbekistan	Hayrapetyan, Susanna	SIL	FY05	40.00	46.79
P074841	Bangladesh—Health Nutrition and Population Sector Program	IBRD/IDA	Bangladesh	Alam, Bushra Binte	SIML	FY05	300.00	350.89
P075058	India: Tamil Nadu Health Systems Project	IBRD/IDA	India	Gopalan, Sundararajan Srinivasa	SIL	FY05	110.83	129.63

table continues next page

108

B.3 Projects Likely to Benefit Young Children (Lending and Trust Funded) *(continued)*

Project ID	Product line	Project name	Country	TTL	Lending instrument	Approval year	Total lending amount (US$, nominal)	Total lending amount, US$ (2013)
P076799	IBRD/IDA	ST. VINCENT SNF THE GRENADINES HIV/AIDS PREVENTION AND CONTROL	St. Vincent and the Grenadines	Pena, Christine Lao	APL	FY05	7.00	8.19
P078991	IBRD/IDA	Health Services Extension and Modernization (2nd APL)	Nicaragua	Bortman, Carlos Marcelo	APL	FY05	11.00	12.87
P079628	IBRD/IDA	Second Women's Health and Safe Motherhood	Philippines	Chakraborty, Sarbani	SIL	FY05	16.00	18.71
P080413	IBRD/IDA	Great Lakes Initiative on HIV/AIDS (GLIA) Support	Africa	Kantabaze, Pamphile	APL	FY05	20.00	23.39
P082613	IBRD/IDA	Regional HIV/AIDS Treatment Acceleration Project	Africa	Voetberg, Albertus	SIL	FY05	59.80	69.94
P083180	IBRD/IDA	HIV/AIDS, Malaria and TB Control Project (HAMSET)	Angola	Cossa, Humberto Albino	SIL	FY05	21.00	24.56
P083401	IBRD/IDA	Health Sector Reform Project	Malawi	Dutta, Sheila	SIML	FY05	15.00	17.54
P087843	IBRD/IDA	HIV and AIDS Capacity Building and Technical Assistance Project	Lesotho	Zhao, Feng	TAL	FY05	5.00	5.85
P090652	IBRD/IDA	Partnership for Polio Eradication Project Supplemental Credit	Nigeria	Govindaraj, Ramesh	SIL	FY05	51.70	60.47
P091365	IBRD/IDA	Social Sector Programmatic Development Policy Credit II (SSPC II)	Bolivia	Walker, David Ian	DPL	FY05	15.00	17.54

table continues next page

B.3 Projects Likely to Benefit Young Children (Lending and Trust Funded) *(continued)*

Project ID	Project name	Product line	Country	TTL	Lending instrument	Approval year	Total lending amount (US$, nominal)	Total lending amount, US$ (2013)
P094694	Eritrea HIV/AIDS/STI, TB, Malaria and Reproductive Health Project (HAMSET II)	IBRD/IDA	Eritrea	Mohammed-Roberts, Rianna L.	SIL	FY05	24.00	28.07
P074027	Health Services Improvement Project	IBRD/IDA	Lao PDR	Chanthala, Phetdara	SIL	FY06	15.00	16.98
P075464	National Sector Support for Health Reform	IBRD/IDA	Philippines	Rosadia, Roberto Antonio F.	SIML	FY06	110.00	124.52
P076658	Lesotho: Health Sector Reform Project Phase 2	IBRD/IDA	Lesotho	Zhao, Feng	APL	FY06	6.50	7.36
P078978	Community and Basic Health Project	IBRD/IDA	Tajikistan	Msisha, Wezi Marianne	SIL	FY06	10.00	11.32
P082056	Paraguay Mother and Child Basic Health Insurance	IBRD/IDA	Paraguay	Lavadenz, Fernando	SIL	FY06	22.00	24.90
P083350	Instit. Strengthening and Health Sector Support Program (ISHSSP)	IBRD/IDA	Niger	Karamoko, Djibrilla	SIML	FY06	35.00	39.62
P084977	Health and Social Protection Project	IBRD/IDA	Kyrgyz Republic	Jaganjac, Nedim	SIL	FY06	15.00	16.98
P088797	Multisectoral HIV/AIDS Program	IBRD/IDA	Ghana	Saleh, Karima	SIL	FY06	20.00	22.64
P090615	Second Multisectoral STI/HIV/AIDS Prevention project	IBRD/IDA	Madagascar	Qamruddin, Jumana N.	SIL	FY06	30.00	33.96
P093987	Health Sector Support & Multisectoral AIDS Project	IBRD/IDA	Burkina Faso	Ousmane Diadie, Haidara	SIML	FY06	47.70	54.00

table continues next page

B.3 Projects Likely to Benefit Young Children (Lending and Trust Funded) *(continued)*

Project ID	Project name	Product line	Country	TTL	Lending instrument	Approval year	Total lending amount (US$, nominal)	Total lending amount, US$ (2013)
P094278	Health and Nutrition Support Project	IBRD/IDA	Mauritania	Magazi, Ibrahim	SIL	FY06	10.00	11.32
P096131	Zambia Malaria Booster Project	IBRD/IDA	Zambia	Vledder, Monique	SIL	FY06	20.00	22.64
P096482	BENIN: Malaria Control Booster Program	IBRD/IDA	Benin	D'Almeida, Ayite-Fily	SIL	FY06	31.00	35.09
P097402	Pakistan: Second Partnership for Polio Eradication Project	IBRD/IDA	Pakistan	Haq, Inaam	SIL	FY06	46.70	52.87
P071160	India: Karnataka Health Systems	IBRD/IDA	India	Mullen, Patrick M.	SIL	FY07	141.83	156.08
P075060	India: Reproductive and Child Health Second Phase	IBRD/IDA	India	Rajan, Vikram Sundara	SIL	FY07	360.00	396.17
P090993	AR—Essential Public Health Functions	IBRD/IDA	Argentina	Lavadenz, Fernando	SIL	FY07	220.00	242.10
P095250	Health Services and Social Assistance	IBRD/IDA	Moldova	Belli, Paolo	SIL	FY07	17.00	18.71
P096198	Multisector Demographic Project	IBRD/IDA	Niger	Karamoko, Djibrilla	SIL	FY07	10.00	11.00
P097921	Malaria Control Booster Project	IBRD/IDA	Nigeria	Nair, Dinesh M.	SIL	FY07	180.00	198.08
P098031	Second Multisectoral HIV/AIDS Project	IBRD/IDA	Ethiopia	Kamil, Mohamed Ali	SIL	FY07	30.00	33.01
P098792	Health Sector Support Project—Additional Financing	IBRD/IDA	Malawi	Dutta, Sheila	SIML	FY07	5.00	5.50

table continues next page

B.3 Projects Likely to Benefit Young Children (Lending and Trust Funded) *(continued)*

Project ID	Project name	Product line	Country	TTL	Lending instrument	Approval year	Total lending amount (US$, nominal)	Total lending amount, US$ (2013)
P103606	Madagascar Sustainable Health System Development Project	IBRD/IDA	Madagascar	Sharp, Maryanne	SIL	FY07	10.00	11.00
P104189	Multisectoral HIV/AIDS Project—Additional Financing	IBRD/IDA	Rwanda	Schneidman, Miriam	SIL	FY07	10.00	11.00
P104900	Pakistan: Additional Financing for the Second Partnership for Polio Eradication Project	IBRD/IDA	Pakistan	Haq, Inaam	SIL	FY07	21.14	23.26
P105282	Liberia Health Systems Reconstruction	IBRD/IDA	Liberia	Mohammed-Roberts, Rianna L.	ERL	FY07	8.50	9.35
P104523	IGAD Regional HIV/AIDS Partnership Program (IRAPP) Support Project	REA	Africa	Bertoncino, Carla	SIL	FY07	15.00	16.51
P050716	UY Noncommunicable Diseases Prevention Project	IBRD/IDA	Uruguay	Perez, Luis Orlando	SIL	FY08	25.30	27.25
P071631	Emergency Multisector HIV/AIDS Project	IBRD/IDA	Cote d'Ivoire	Magazi, Ibrahim	ERL	FY08	20.00	21.54
P083997	Alto Solimoes Basic Services and Sustainable Development Project in Support of the Zona Franca Verde Program	IBRD/IDA	Brazil	Debroux, Laurent	APL	FY08	24.25	26.12

table continues next page

B.3 Projects Likely to Benefit Young Children (Lending and Trust Funded) *(continued)*

Project ID	Project name	Product line	Country	TTL	Lending instrument	Approval year	Total lending amount (US$, nominal)	Total lending amount, US$ (2013)
P095626	Second Family Health Extension Adaptable Lending	IBRD/IDA	Brazil	Dmytraczenko, Tania	APL	FY08	83.45	89.89
P102284	Cambodia Second Health Sector Support Program	IBRD/IDA	Cambodia	Johnston, Timothy A.	SIL	FY08	30.00	32.32
P104525	Cameroon Health Sector Support Investment (SWAP)	IBRD/IDA	Cameroon	Sorgho, Gaston	SIL	FY08	25.00	26.93
P105093	TZ-Health Sector Development II Scale-Up	IBRD/IDA	Tanzania	Haazen, Dominic S.	APL	FY08	60.00	64.63
P106622	Jamaica Second HIV/AIDS Project	IBRD/IDA	Jamaica	Chao, Shiyan	SIL	FY08	10.00	10.77
P106851	Health Sector Services Development	IBRD/IDA	Congo, Rep.	Frere, Jean-Jacques	SIL	FY08	40.00	43.09
P109964	Second Multisectoral HIV/AIDS	IBRD/IDA	Burundi	Kantabaze, Pamphile	SIL	FY08	15.00	16.16
P110731	Nepal—Health Sector Program Project Additional Financing	IBRD/IDA	Nepal	Voetberg, Albertus	SIML	FY08	50.00	53.86
P110815	Health Sector Support and AIDS project—Additional Financing	IBRD/IDA	Burkina Faso	Ousmane Diadie, Haidara	SIML	FY08	15.00	16.16
P094360	India: National Vector Borne Disease Control and Polio Eradication Support Project	IBRD/IDA	India	Govindaraj, Ramesh	SIL	FY09	521.00	552.17

table continues next page

B.3 Projects Likely to Benefit Young Children (Lending and Trust Funded) (continued)

Project ID	Project name	Product line	Country	TTL	Lending instrument	Approval year	Total lending amount (US$, nominal)	Total lending amount, US$ (2013)
P099930	Health Service Delivery	IBRD/IDA	Mozambique	Cossa, Humberto Albino	SIL	FY09	44.60	47.27
P107843	Federal District Multisector Management	IBRD/IDA	Brazil	Silveira, Ricardo Rocha	SIL	FY09	130.00	137.78
P110696	Partnership for Polio Eradication Project—Additional Financing (FY08)	IBRD/IDA	Nigeria	Nair, Dinesh M.	SIL	FY09	50.00	52.99
P110697	Second Health Systems Development II—Additional Financing	IBRD/IDA	Nigeria	Govindaraj, Ramesh	SIL	FY09	90.00	95.38
P113489	Additional Financing of Health Sector Development	IBRD/IDA	Sri Lanka	Gopalan, Sundararajan Srinivasa	SIL	FY09	24.00	25.44
P114508	Pakistan: Third Partnership for Polio Eradication Project	IBRD/IDA	Pakistan	Navaratne, Kumari Vinodhani	SIL	FY09	74.68	79.15
P115036	Malaria Control Booster Project—Additional Financing	IBRD/IDA	Nigeria	Nair, Dinesh M.	SIL	FY09	100.00	105.98
P115801	Community and Basic Health Project—Additional Financing	IBRD/IDA	Tajikistan	Msisha, Wezi Marianne	SIL	FY09	5.00	5.30
P116637	HIV/AIDS and Health—Additional Financing	IBRD/IDA	Congo, Rep.	Louani, Mahamat Goadi	SIL	FY09	5.00	5.30
P074091	Health Sector Support	IBRD/IDA	Kenya	Ramana, Gandham N.V.	SIL	FY10	100.00	105.43

table continues next page

B.3 Projects Likely to Benefit Young Children (Lending and Trust Funded) *(continued)*

Project ID	Project name	Product line	Country	TTL	Lending instrument	Approval year	Total lending amount (US$, nominal)	Total lending amount, US$ (2013)
P095275	Central North Region Health Support Project	IBRD/IDA	Vietnam	Hurt, Kari L.	SIL	FY10	65.00	68.53
P105724	Population and HIV AIDS Additional Financing	IBRD/IDA	Chad	Cisse, Boubou	SIL	FY10	20.00	21.09
P106619	Health Sector Reform Second Phase APL (PARSS 2)	IBRD/IDA	Dominican Republic	Pena, Christine Lao	APL	FY10	30.50	32.16
P113113	Social Sector Support (Additional Financing)	IBRD/IDA	São Tomé and Príncipe	Martins, Geraldo Joao	SIL	FY10	2.10	2.21
P113896	AR San Juan SWAP	IBRD/IDA	Argentina	Fiess, Norbert Matthias	SIL	FY10	50.00	52.72
P118830	Tamil Nadu Health Additional Financing	IBRD/IDA	India	Gopalan, Sundararajan Srinivasa	SIL	FY10	117.70	124.09
P119067	Tanzania Health Sector Development Project II—Additional Financing FY10	IBRD/IDA	Tanzania	Haazen, Dominic S.	APL	FY10	40.00	42.17
P120565	Afghanistan—Support to Basic Package of Health Services (Strengthening Health Activity for Rural Poor	REA	Afghanistan	Haq, Inaam	SIL	FY10	17.90	18.87
P106735	Provincial Public Health Insurance Development Project	IBRD/IDA	Argentina	Cortez, Rafael A.	SIL	FY11	400.00	414.31

table continues next page

B.3 Projects Likely to Benefit Young Children (Lending and Trust Funded) *(continued)*

Project ID	Project name	Product line	Country	TTL	Lending instrument	Approval year	Total lending amount (US$, nominal)	Total lending amount, US$ (2013)
P106870	Improving Community and Family Health Care Services Project	IBRD/IDA	Nicaragua	Gordillo-Tobar, Amparo Elena	SIL	FY11	21.00	21.75
P110156	Swaziland Health, HIV/AIDS and TB Project	IBRD/IDA	Swaziland	Yamashita-Allen, Kanako	SIL	FY11	20.00	20.72
P110599	Essential Public Health Functions Programs II Project	IBRD/IDA	Argentina	Lavadenz, Fernando	SIL	FY11	461.00	477.50
P113349	Health System Improvement Project	IBRD/IDA	Uzbekistan	Hayrapetyan, Susanna	SIL	FY11	93.00	96.33
P116167	HIV/AIDS Support Project 2	IBRD/IDA	Niger	Karamoko, Djibrilla	SIL	FY11	20.00	20.72
P120872	Malaria Booster Project Additional financing	IBRD/IDA	Zambia	Vledder, Monique	SIL	FY11	30.00	31.07
P124264	Partnership for Polio Eradication Project—3rd Additional Financing (FY11)	IBRD/IDA	Nigeria	Nair, Dinesh M.	SIL	FY11	60.00	62.15
P125109	Pakistan—Third Partnership for Polio Eradication Project—AF	IBRD/IDA	Pakistan	Navaratne, Kumari Vinodhani	SIL	FY11	41.00	42.47
P125285	Health Sector Support and Multisectoral Aids Project—Additional Financing	IBRD/IDA	Burkina Faso	Ousmane Diadie, Haidara	SIML	FY11	36.00	37.29

table continues next page

B.3 Projects Likely to Benefit Young Children (Lending and Trust Funded) *(continued)*

Project ID	Project name	Product line	Country	TTL	Lending instrument	Approval year	Total lending amount (US$, nominal)	Total lending amount, US$ (2013)
P126426	Pakistan: Revitalizing Health Services in KP	REA	Pakistan	Masud, Tayyeb	ERL	FY12	70.00	71.15
P127187	South Sudan Health Rapid Results Project	Special Financing	South Sudan	Bakilana, Anne Margreth	ERL	FY12	28.00	28.46
P129663	Afghanistan: System Enhancement for Health Action in Transition Project	IBRD/IDA	Afghanistan	Sayed, Ghulam Dastagir	ERL	FY13	100.00	100.00
P132541	Second Additional Financing for Third Partnership for Polio Eradication Project	IBRD/IDA	Pakistan	Masud, Tayyeb	SIL	FY13	24.00	24.00
P128442	Disease Prevention and Control Project	IBRD/IDA	Armenia	Msisha, Wezi Marianne	SIL	FY13	35.00	35.00
P128909	Liberia Health Systems Strengthening	IBRD/IDA	Liberia	Mohammed-Roberts, Rianna L.	SIL	FY13	10.00	10.00
P130395	India: Karnataka Health Systems Additional Financing	IBRD/IDA	India	Mullen, Patrick M.	SIL	FY13	70.00	70.00
P130865	NG-Polio Eradication Support (FY13)	IBRD/IDA	Nigeria	Mabuchi, Shunsuke	SIL	FY13	95.00	95.00
P129652	Development Policies for the State of Sergipe	IBRD/IDA	Brazil	Dmytraczenko, Tania	DPL	FY13	150.00	150.00
P144537	HIV/AIDS Prevention Additional Financing	REA	Vietnam	Nguyen, Mai Thi	SIL	FY13	9.38	9.38

table continues next page

B.3 Projects Likely to Benefit Young Children (Lending and Trust Funded) *(continued)*

Project ID	Project name	Product line	Country	TTL	Lending instrument	Approval year	Total lending amount (US$, nominal)	Total lending amount, US$ (2013)
P144040	Second Additional Financing to the North Sudan Decentralized Health System Development Project	REA	Sudan	Soares, Isabel Cristina	SIL	FY13	2.00	2.00
P144520	Health Sector Strategic Plan Support Additional Financing	REA	Timor-Leste	Sullivan, Eileen Brainne	SIL	FY13	17.70	17.70
Social Protection								
P064536	Child Welfare Reform Project	IBRD/IDA	Bulgaria	Gotcheva, Boryana	SIL	FY01	8.00	10.21
P064906	Poverty Reduction and Local Development Project	IBRD/IDA	Nicaragua	Coudouel, Aline	SIL	FY01	60.00	76.60
P067774	Social Safety Net Project	IBRD/IDA	Jamaica	Tesliuc, Cornelia M.	SIL	FY02	40.00	50.16
P073817	Programmatic Social Reform Loan Project (02)	IBRD/IDA	Peru	Rofman, Rafael P.	SAL	FY03	100.00	123.22
P075911	Third Social Action Fund (MASAF III)	IBRD/IDA	Malawi	Lenneiye, Nginya Mungai	APL	FY03	60.00	73.93
P079335	SL-National Social Action Project	IBRD/IDA	Sierra Leone	Van Dyck, John	SIL	FY03	35.00	43.13
P082700	BO Social Safety Net SAC	IBRD/IDA	Bolivia	Salazar, Manuel	SAL	FY03	35.00	43.13
P077739	Poverty Reduction Support Credit 2 (PRSC 2)	IBRD/IDA	Albania	Goldman, Philip S.	PRSC	FY04	18.00	21.69
P079060	CO: Programmatic Labor Reform and Social Structural Adjustment Loan	IBRD/IDA	Colombia	Paqueo, Vicente B.	SAL	FY04	200.00	240.99

table continues next page

B.3 Projects Likely to Benefit Young Children (Lending and Trust Funded) *(continued)*

Project ID	Project name	Product line	Country	TTL	Lending instrument	Approval year	Total lending amount (US$, nominal)	Total lending amount, US$ (2013)
P085433	Dominican Republic Social Crisis Response Adjustment Loan	IBRD/IDA	Dominican Republic	Carlson, Samuel C.	SAL	FY04	100.00	120.50
P082865	CO: Programmatic Labor Reform and Social Structural Adjustment Loan2	IBRD/IDA	Colombia	Cunningham, Wendy	SAL	FY05	200.00	233.93
P083968	PE-Programmatic Social Reform Loan IV	IBRD/IDA	Peru	Rofman, Rafael P.	DPL	FY05	100.00	116.96
P095028	Uruguay Social Program Support Loan	IBRD/IDA	Uruguay	Rofman, Rafael P.	DPL	FY05	75.38	88.17
P089443	CO Social Safety Net Project	IBRD/IDA	Colombia	Jones, Theresa	SIL	FY06	86.40	97.81
P098167	(APL1) Bono de Desarrollo Humano	IBRD/IDA	Ecuador	Warren, David Seth	APL	FY06	60.00	67.92
P094097	CO-3rd Prog. Labor Reform and Social Development Policy Loan	IBRD/IDA	Colombia	Cunningham, Wendy	DPL	FY07	200.00	220.09
P094225	Social Investment Fund III	IBRD/IDA	Armenia	Drabek, Ivan	SIL	FY07	25.00	27.51
P101086	Results and Accoutability (RECAT) DPL	IBRD/IDA	-Peru	Walker, David Ian	DPL	FY07	150.00	165.07
P101950	HIV/AIDS MAP Supplemental	IBRD/IDA	Cape Verde	Ovadiya, Mirey	SIL	FY07	5.00	5.50
P104507	Additional Financing for Colombia Social Safety Net Project (Ln. 7337)	IBRD/IDA	Colombia	Jones, Theresa	SIL	FY07	104.80	115.33

table continues next page

B.3 Projects Likely to Benefit Young Children (Lending and Trust Funded) *(continued)*

Project ID	Project name	Product line	Country	TTL	Lending instrument	Approval year	Total lending amount (US$, nominal)	Total lending amount, US$ (2013)
P090010	DO Social Sectors Investment Program	IBRD/IDA	Dominican Republic	Fruttero, Anna	SIL	FY08	19.40	20.90
P100546	Jordan Social Protection Enhancement Project	IBRD/IDA	Jordan	Ersado, Lire	SIL	FY08	4.00	4.31
P105024	Social Protection Project	IBRD/IDA	Jamaica	Lamanna, Francesca	SIL	FY08	40.00	43.09
P090644	Community and Social Development Project	IBRD/IDA	Nigeria	Okunmadewa, Foluso	SIL	FY09	200.00	211.96
P101177	Second Results and Accountability (RE-CAT) Development Policy Loan-Deferred Drawdown Option	IBRD/IDA	Peru	Marini, Alessandra	DPL	FY09	330.00	349.74
P102119	Nigeria HIV/AIDS Program Development Project II	IBRD/IDA	Nigeria	Akala, Francisca Ayodeji	SIL	FY09	225.00	238.46
P103160	Pakistan: Social Safety Net Project	IBRD/IDA	Pakistan	Vermehren, Andrea	SIL	FY09	60.00	63.59
P106332	Bangladesh Disability and Children at Risk	IBRD/IDA	Bangladesh	Leino, Jessica Leigh	SIL	FY09	35.00	37.09
P106834	RW-First Community Living Standards Grant	IBRD/IDA	Rwanda	Kamurase, Alex	DPL	FY09	6.00	6.36
P111545	Kenya Cash Transfer for Orphans and Vulnerable Children	IBRD/IDA	Kenya	Wiseman, William David	SIL	FY09	50.00	52.99
P115067	Support to Oportunidades Project	IBRD/IDA	Mexico	Theresa Jones	SIL	FY09	1503.76	1593.72

table continues next page

B.3 Projects Likely to Benefit Young Children (Lending and Trust Funded) *(continued)*

Project ID	Project name	Product line	Country	TTL	Lending instrument	Approval year	Total lending amount (US$, nominal)	Total lending amount, US$ (2013)
P116125	Poland Employment, Entrepreneurship and Human Capital Dev. Policy Program DPL	IBRD/IDA	Poland	Packard, Truman G.	DPL	FY09	1300.24	1378.02
P082144	PH-Social Welfare and Development Reform	IBRD/IDA	Philippines	Chaudhury, Nazmul	SIL	FY10	405.00	427.00
P107416	Expanding Opportunities for Vunerable Groups	IBRD/IDA	Guatemala	Blanco, Gaston Mariano	SIL	FY10	114.50	120.72
P114774	Social Protection TA Additional Financing	IBRD/IDA	Chile	Jones, Theresa	TAL	FY10	3.00	3.16
P115592	Social Protection	IBRD/IDA	Honduras	Acosta, Pablo Ariel	SIL	FY10	40.00	42.17
P115732	Latvia First Special Development Policy Loan: Safety Net and Social Sector Reform Program	IBRD/IDA	Latvia	Packard, Truman G.	DPL	FY10	143.90	151.72
P116369	DO Additional Financing Social Sectors Investment Progr	IBRD/IDA	Dominican Republic	Fruttero, Anna	SIL	FY10	10.00	10.54
P116972	First Performance and Accountability of Social Sectors Development Policy Loan	IBRD/IDA	Dominican Republic	Clert, Carine	DPL	FY10	150.00	158.15
P117758	Rwanda Second Community Living Standards Grant	IBRD/IDA	Rwanda	Staines, Verdon S.	DPL	FY10	6.00	6.33
P117949	RY:Social Fund for Development IV	IBRD/IDA	Yemen, Rep.	Hong, Mira	SIL	FY10	60.00	63.26

table continues next page

B.3 Projects Likely to Benefit Young Children (Lending and Trust Funded) *(continued)*

Project ID	Project name	Product line	Country	TTL	Lending instrument	Approval year	Total lending amount (US$, nominal)	Total lending amount, US$ (2013)
P101504	Second Bolsa Famlia	IBRD/IDA	Brazil	Steta Gandara, Maria Concepcion	APL	FY11	200.00	207.16
P116264	Third Results and Accountability (REACT) Programmatic DPL	IBRD/IDA	Peru	Marini, Alessandra	DPL	FY11	50.00	51.79
P121673	Social Assistance System Modernization Project	IBRD/IDA	Romania	Tesliuc, Emil Daniel	SIL	FY11	710.40	735.82
P121778	Second Performance and Accountability of Social Sectors Development Policy Loan	IBRD/IDA	Dominican Republic	Clert, Carine	DPL	FY11	150.00	155.37
P122157	Rwanda Third Community Living Standards Grant	IBRD/IDA	Rwanda	Kamurase, Alex	DPL	FY11	6.00	6.21
P122349	Additional Financing for the Support to Oportunidades	IBRD/IDA	Mexico	Jones, Theresa	SIL	FY11	1250.00	1294.73
P126158	Additional Financing For Nutrition And Social Protection Project	IBRD/IDA	Honduras	McEvoy, Karla J.	SIL	FY11	3.60	3.73
P124045	Tanzania Productive Social Safety Net	IBRD/IDA	Tanzania	Manjolo, Ida	APL	FY12	220.00	223.62
P131028	PE Social Inclusion DPL	IBRD/IDA	Peru	Rofman, Rafael P.	DPL	FY13	45.00	45.00
P131029	PE Social Inclusion TAL	IBRD/IDA	Peru	Marini, Alessandra	TAL	FY13	10.00	10.00
P133699	Additional Financing for Social Fund for Development IV	IBRD/IDA	Yemen, Rep.	Hong, Mira	SIL	FY13	25.00	25.00
P133811	Emergency Crisis Recovery Project	IBRD/IDA	Yemen, Rep	Ersado, Lire	ERL	FY13	100.00	100.00

table continues next page

B.3 Projects Likely to Benefit Young Children (Lending and Trust Funded) (continued)

Project ID	Project name	Product line	Country	TTL	Lending instrument	Approval year	Total lending amount (US$, nominal)	Total lending amount, US$ (2013)
P124761	Social Promotion And Protection Project	IBRD/IDA	Lebanon	Sayed, Haneen Ismail	SIL	FY13	30.00	30.00
P126964	Nigeria Youth Employment and Social Support Operation	IBRD/IDA	Nigeria	Okunmadewa, Foluso	SIL	FY13	300.00	300.00
P128534	Cameroon Social Safety Nets	IBRD/IDA	Cameroon	Del Ninno, Carlo	SIL	FY13	50.00	50.00
P143915	Safety Net and Skills Development	IBRD/IDA	South Sudan	Gossa, Endashaw Tadesse	IPF	FY13	21.00	21.00
P128891	Ethiopia Promoting Basic Services Program Phase III Project	IBRD/IDA	Ethiopia	Khan, Qaiser M.	SIML	FY13	600.00	600.00
P144618	Integration of Children with Disabilities into Mainstream Schools	REA	Moldova	Smolyar, Yuliya	SIL	FY13	2.86	2.86

Note: APL = Adaptable Program Loan; DPL = Development Policy Loan; ERL = Emergency Recovery Loan; FY = fiscal year; IBRD = International Bank for Reconstruction and Development; IDA = International Development Association; IPF = Investment Project Financing; PRSC = Poverty Reduction Support Credit; REA = Recipient Executed Activity; SAL = Special Assistance Loan; SIL = Specific Investment Loan; SIML = Sector Investment and Maintenance Loan; TAL = Technical Assistance Loan; TTL = Task Team Leader.

APPENDIX C

Snapshot of Case Studies of Operations

Table C.1 Snapshot of Case Studies of Operations

BULGARIA: SOCIAL INCLUSION PROJECT	P100657
PROJECT DEVELOPMENT OBJECTIVE:	To promote social inclusion through increasing the school readiness of children below the age of seven, targeting low-income and marginalized families (including children with a disability and other special needs)
COMPONENTS:	1. **Integrated social and childcare services** (U$39.6 million) 1.1. Programs for children aged 0–3 and their parents 1.2. Programs for children aged 3–6 and their parents 1.3. Infrastructure and material investments 1.4. Training for service providers 2. **Capacity building** (US$0.7 million) 2.1. Local project management capacity building 2.2. Impact evaluation 2.3. Audit and implementation support
PROJECT DEVELOPMENT OBJECTIVE INDICATORS:	1. Share of vulnerable children aged 6 who pass school readiness diagnostic test 2. Number of children aged 3–6 newly enrolled in kindergartens and preschool groups 3. Number of children with disabilities and other special needs enrolled in mainstream kindergartens and preschool groups
SECTOR BOARD	Social protection
STATUS	Active
DURATION	Seven years (FY09–FY16)
BORROWER	Republic of Bulgaria
TOTAL PROJECT COST	US$43 million
FUNDING	IBRD loan: US$43 million
LENDING INSTRUMENT	Specific Investment Loan
TARGET POPULATION	15,000 children below the age of 7 and their parents, targeting low-income and marginalized
PARTNER AGENCIES	Ministry of Labor and Social Policy
WB PROJECT MANAGER	Christain Bodewig, Peter Pojarski, Plamen Danchev
MOST RECENT ISR RESULTS	Progress toward achievement of PDO: *Moderately Unsatisfactory* Overall Implementation Progress: *Moderately Satisfactory* (as of December 2013)

table continues next page

(continued)

BULGARIA: SOCIAL INCLUSION PROJECT	**P100657**
EXPECTED RESULTS	• Improved parenting skills (suggested for revision under possible restructuring) • Increased enrollment rate in mainstream preschool and kindergarten among children below the age of seven from low-income and marginalized families • Increased enrollment rate of children with disability in mainstream preschool, kindergarten, and childcare centers • Increased number of new childcare places created through project (As of 2012, 95 of municipalities completed construction) • Increased number of kindergarten and childcare facilities, staff having received training

Sources: PAD (October 2008); ISRs (June 2011, November 2012, December 2013); Social Inclusion Project, Operations Manual (November 2010); Personal communication with Plamen Danchev (TTL), (November, 2012).
Note: FY = fiscal year; IBRD = International Bank for Reconstruction and Development; ISR = Implementation Status and Results; PDO = project development objective; WB = World Bank.

Eritrea: INTEGRATED EARLY CHILDHOOD DEVELOPMENT PROJECT	**P068463**
PROJECT DEVELOPMENT OBJECTIVE:	To promote the healthy growth and holistic development of Eritrean children
COMPONENTS:	1. **Improve child health** (US$10.5 million) 2. **Child and maternal nutrition** (US$4.6 million) 3. **Early childhood care and education** (US$11.8 million) 4. **Support of children in need of special protection measures** (US$11.7 million) 5. **Project management, evaluation, and strategic communication** (US$5.4 million) 5.1. Project Management Team for overall project management and coordination 5.2. Advocacy and awareness for ECD issues 5.3. Innovation Fund to support new activities at local level 5.4. Integrated ECD program evaluation/survey and research
PROJECT DEVELOPMENT OBJECTIVE INDICATORS:	1. Case fatality rate (CFR) in under six children from combined major causes (malaria, acute respiratory infections, diarrhea, measles, anemia/malnutrition) 2. Percentage of underweight children under 3 years 3. Repetition and dropout rates from primary grade 1 to grade 2 4. Successful reunification of orphans with nearest relatives
SECTOR BOARD	Education
STATUS	Closed
DURATION	Seven years (FY01–FY07)
BORROWER	Government of Eritrea
TOTAL PROJECT COST	US$49 million
FUNDING	IDA Credit: US$40 million; Government of Eritrea: US$4 million; Government of Italy: US$5 million; Government of Netherlands (Netherland's Partnership Trust Fund): US$19,500; Government of France (Consultant Trust Fund): US$18,200

table continues next page

(continued)

Eritrea: INTEGRATED EARLY CHILDHOOD DEVELOPMENT PROJECT	**P068463**
LENDING INSTRUMENT	Specific Investment Loan
TARGET POPULATION	560,000 children under six years of age
PARTNER AGENCIES	Ministry of Education, Ministry of Local Government, Ministry of Health, Ministry of Labor and Human Welfare, Ministry of Agriculture, Ministry of Fisheries, Government of Italy
WB PROJECT MANAGERS	Susan E. Hirshberg, Christopher D. Walker, Marito Garcia
ICR RATINGS	Outcomes: *Satisfactory* Risk to Development Outcome: *Substantial* Bank Performance: *Satisfactory* Borrower Performance: *Satisfactory* (May 2007)
RESULTS	• Reduced case fatality rate in under-6 children from combined major causes: malaria, ARI, diarrhea, measles, and anemia (cumulative reduction 53.4) • Decreased repetition and dropout rates from primary grade 1 and 2 (30 reduction in repetition and 35 reduction in dropout rates) • 31,556 orphans reunified with nearest relatives • 1,096 health workers trained in ICMI case management • 8,667 mothers trained in food security and nutrition • Increased cumulative enrollment in kindergartens (31,653) and childcare centers (50,425) • 36 social workers trained (did not meet target)

Sources: PAD (May, 2000); ICR Report (May, 2007); Garcia, Pence, and Evans (2008); Personal Communication with Marito Garcia (TTL).
Note: ECD = early childhood development; ICR = Implementation Completion Results; IDA = International Development Association.

Indonesia: EARLY CHILDHOOD EDUCATION AND DEVELOPMENT PROJECT	**P089479**
PROJECT DEVELOPMENT OBJECTIVE:	*To improve poor children's overall development and readiness for further education, within a sustainable quality ECED system.*
COMPONENTS:	1. **Increase integrated ECED service delivery in targeted poor communities** (US$95.2 million) 1.1. Establish training program and provide staff development 1.2. Precondition and launch competitive grant process 1.3. Provide block grants to poor communities 1.4. Recognize model ECED services and use them for demonstration purposes 2. **Develop sustainable system for ECED quality** (US$12.3 million) 2.1. Quality assurance 2.2. Institutionalization of quality ECED at the district and provincial level 3. **Establish effective project management, monitoring, and evaluation** (US$20.2 million) 3.1. Project Management (at central and district levels) 3.2. Monitoring and Evaluation

table continues next page

(continued)

Indonesia: EARLY CHILDHOOD EDUCATION AND DEVELOPMENT PROJECT	**P089479**
PROJECT DEVELOPMENT OBJECTIVE INDICATORS:	1. Increase in child growth and development score of children 0–3 years [measured by DDTK tool (*deteksi dini tumbuh kembang Anak* "home-based developmental milestones"]
	2. Increase in early development scores of children entering kindergarten or first grade of primary school (EDI adapted for local use)
SECTOR BOARD	Education
STATUS	Active
DURATION	Nine years (FY06–FY14)
BORROWER	Republic of Indonesia
TOTAL PROJECT COST	US$127.7 million
FUNDING	IDA credit: US$67.5 million; Republic of Indonesia: US$34.9 million; Indonesia Free-Standing Trust Fund: US$25.3 million
LENDING INSTRUMENT	Specific Investment Loan
TARGET POPULATION	738,000 children ages 0–6 years and their parents/caretakers in 3,000 poor villages
PARTNER AGENCIES	Ministry of National Education
WB PROJECT MANAGER	Rosfita Roesli, Mae Chu Chang
MOST RECENT ISR RESULTS	*Progress towards achievement of PDO*: Moderately satisfactory
	Overall Implementation Progress: Moderately satisfactory
	(as of December 2013)
EXPECTED RESULTS:	• Increased enrollment in ECED services by poor children (673,000 of 738,000 target as of mid 2013)
	• Impact study of operation baseline 2009, midline 2010, endline 2013)
	• Targeted villages submit routine reports to districts (achieved as of 2011)
	• Targeted villages undertake annual community assessments (80% of 3,000 villages as of 2013)
	• Targeted districts have qualified and functioning district training teams (achieved as of 2011)
	• Standards developed and recognition of models in ECED centers (achieved as of 2011)
	• Targeted districts have regulations supporting ECED positions in district government (70 as of 2011)
	• Block grants awarded to communities (achieved as of 2013)
	• Communities submit expression of interest to receive grants for ECED service development (achieved as of 2013)
	• Parents and communities receive information regarding ECED (achieved as of 2011)

Sources: PAD (May, 2006); Grant Reporting and Monitoring Report(August, 2011); ISRs (April 2011, January 2011); Knowledge Brief: A Snapshot of Early Childhood Development in Indonesia (2010); Hasan, Hyson, and Chang (2012); Personal communication with Amer Hasan and Rosfita Roesli (November, 2012).
Note: ECED = early childhood education and development; EDI = Early Development Instrument; IDA = International Development Association; ISR = Implementation Status and Results.

Jamaica: EARLY CHILDHOOD DEVELOPMENT PROJECT	P095673
PROJECT DEVELOPMENT OBJECTIVE:	To support the objectives of the National Strategic Plan to: (i) improve the monitoring of children's development, the screening of household-level risks, and the risk mitigation and early intervention systems; (ii) enhance the quality of early childhood schools and care facilities; and (iii) strengthen early childhood organizations and institutions.
COMPONENTS:	1. **Cofinancing the implementation of the National Strategy Plan under SWAp modalities** (US$13.1 million) 1.1. Parenting education and support 1.2. Preventative health care 1.3. Screening, diagnosis, and early intervention 1.4. Safe, learner-centered facilities; trained practitioners 1.5. Governance 1.6. Evidence-based decision making 2. **Technical Assistance under Standard Financing Arrangements—support development of national policy on screening, referral, and early intervention** (US$1.9 million)
PROJECT DEVELOPMENT OBJECTIVE INDICATORS:	1. Number of children below 3 monitored and screened for risks using child health passport 2. Health centers offering well-child clinics that are accredited 3. PATH beneficiary households with children 0–6 years old screened for child development risks 4. Parents/guardians of children 0–6 years old who have ever received information on parenting 5. Children enrolled in early childhood institutions who attend schools that have permits to operate
SECTOR BOARD	Education
STATUS	Active
DURATION	(11 years) FY08–FY19
BORROWER	Ministry of Finance and the Public Service
TOTAL PROJECT COST	US$508.9 million
FUNDING	IBRD loan: US$15 million; Borrower: US$493.9 million (Additional financing in FY14 for $12 million IBRD loan and $2 million borrower)
LENDING INSTRUMENT	Specific Investment Loan
TARGET POPULATION	All Jamaican children below six years old and their parents
PARTNER AGENCIES	Early Childhood Commission of Jamaica,
WB PROJECT MANAGERS	Harriet Nannyonjo, Christoph Kurowski
MOST RECENT ISR RATINGS	Progress toward achievement of PDO: *Moderately Unsatisfactory* Overall Implementation Progress: *Moderately Satisfactory*

table continues next page

(continued)

Jamaica: EARLY CHILDHOOD DEVELOPMENT PROJECT	P095673
EXPECTED RESULTS	• 100 of children below three years monitored and screened for risks using child health passport (achieved as of FY12) • Increased percentage of health centers offering well-child clinics that are accredited • Increased percentage of PATH beneficiary households with children 0–6 years old that are screened for child development risks using screening and documentation model for high risk house • Increased percentage of parents/guardians of children 0–6 years old who have ever received information on parenting, excluding information received from family members and friends • 38 of children enrolled in ECIs that attend schools that have permits to operate (FY14 target is 40) • Increased percentage of ECCE practitioners who receive wage subsidies that are licensed

Sources: PAD (April, 2008); ISRs (August, 2011; September, 2012); Personal Communication with Harriet Nannyonjo (TTL) (November, 2012).
Note: ECCE = early childhood care and education; IBRD = International Bank for Reconstruction and Development; PDO = Project Development Objective; SWAp = Sector-Wide Approach.

JORDAN: ECD COMPONENT OF EDUCATION REFORM FOR KNOWLEDGE ECONOMY I AND II	P075829; P105036
OVERALL PROJECT DEVELOPMENT OBJECTIVE:	*Transform the education system at the early childhood, basic and secondary levels to produce graduates with the skills necessary for the knowledge economy.*
ECD COMPONENT:	*To enhance equity through public provision to kindergarten II (KGII) to low-income areas (Phase I)*
	To expand access and enhance the quality of the ECD program in order to maximize children's learning potential (Phase II)
ECD COMPONENT AND SUBCOMPONENTS:	**Component 4: Promote Readiness for learning through ECE (out of 4) (from Phase I)** 4.1 Enhanced institutional capacity for ECE 4.2 A cadre of ECE educators 4.3 Increased access to KGs for the poor 4.4 Parent and community participation and partnership
PROJECT DEVELOPMENT OBJECTIVE INDICATORS RELATED TO ECD:	1. Gross enrollment rate in second level of kindergarten
SECTOR BOARD	Education
STATUS	Closed
DURATION	13 years (Phase I: FY03–FY09; Phase II: FY10–FY16)
BORROWER	The Hashemite Kingdom of Jordan
ECD COMPONENT COST	Phase I: US$18.5 million (5% of total project cost); Phase II: US$8.8 million (2% of total cost)

table continues next page

(continued)

JORDAN: ECD COMPONENT OF EDUCATION REFORM FOR KNOWLEDGE ECONOMY I AND II	**P075829; P105036**
FUNDING	IBRD loan: US$6.2 million in Phase I (5 of US$120.0 million of total IBRD funding) (No Bank funding for ECD component in Phase II);
	Other financiers: Government of Jordan; US Agency for International Development (USAID); Arab Fund for Economic and Social Development; Canadian International Development Agency (CIDA); British Department for International Development (DFID); EC: European Investment Bank; Islamic Investment Bank; Japan International Cooperation Agency (JICA); Germany Kreditanstalt fur Wiederaufabau (KFW)
LENDING INSTRUMENT	Sector Investment and Maintenance Loan
TARGET POPULATION	Preschool-aged children, focusing particularly on disadvantaged groups
PARTNER AGENCIES	Ministry of Education; USAID;
WB PROJECT MANAGER	Peter Buckland, Juan Manuel Moreno Olmedilla, Tomomi Miyajima (ECD component)
ICR RATINGS	*Outcomes:* Satisfactory (ECD component received Highly Satisfactory rating)
	Risk to Development Outcome: Moderate
	Bank Performance: Satisfactory
	Borrower Performance: Satisfactory
	(December, 2009)
RESULTS	• Increased enrollment in kindergarten (Target of 51 was fully achieved well before end of project)
	• All kindergarten teachers trained on National Curriculum and pedagogy appropriate for ECE
	• Appropriate regulations and standards for kindergarten developed
	• Governorates piloted four integrated child development centers to serve families and communities in remote and poor areas

Sources: PAD (April, 2003); ICR (December, 2009); Project performance assessment report (June, 2011); Personal communication with Tomomi Miyajima (Education Specialist, November, 2012); "KG Study Report: Monitoring and Evaluation Partnership Project", 2012. USAID and World Education
Note: ECD = early childhood development; ECE = early childhood education; IBRD = International Bank for Reconstruction and Development; KG = Kindergarten; USAID = U.S. Agency for International Development.

MEXICO: ECD COMPONENT IN COMPENSATORY EDUCATION PROJECT	**P101369**
OVERALL PROJECT DEVELOPMENT OBJECTIVE:	*To improve access to improve access to Early Childhood Education services and learning outcomes in the most marginalized municipalities of Mexico.*
ECD COMPONENT:	*To improve the competencies and practices in caring for children and contribute to children's comprehensive development and school readiness*
ECD COMPONENT AND SUBCOMPONENTS:	Component 1: **Early Childhood Development Intervention** (1 out of 3) 1.1. Technical assistance and training to ECD promoters and staff 1.2. Provision of out-of-school training to parents, relatives, and caregivers 1.3. Technical assistance to design training materials
ECD-SPECIFIC PROJECT DEVELOPMENT OBJECTIVE INDICATORS:	1. Number of children 0 to 4 years who attended at least 80% of the sessions of the early childhood development intervention in the 172 target municipalities
SECTOR BOARD	Education
STATUS	Active
DURATION	four years (FY10–FY14)
BORROWER	United Mexican States
ECD COMPONENT COST	US$30 million (18% of Total project cost)
FUNDING	IBRD loan: US$100 million; Government of Mexico: US$66.7 million
LENDING INSTRUMENT	Specific Investment Loan
TARGET POPULATION	58,685 children below 6 years old and their parents (52,670 parents; 1,761 pregnant women)
PARTNER AGENCIES	CONAFE (National Council for Education Development), Secretary of Public Education
WB PROJECT MANAGER	Peter Anthony Holland
MOST RECENT ISR RATINGS	*Progress towards achievement of PDO:* Satisfactory *Overall Implementation Progress:* Moderately Satisfactory (December 2011)
EXPECTED RESULTS	• Increased number of ECD service points that are established and complete the minimum number of sessions provided for by the model • Increased number of fathers and mothers trained, that is, who attend at least 80% of the total number of sessions of the ECD model • Increased number of pregnant women trained, that is, who attended at least 80% of the total number of sessions of the ECD model specific to pregnant women • Increased number of fathers trained, that is, who attended at least 80% of the sessions of the ECD model specific to fathers • Establishment and application of instrument that measures competencies of parents and children age 0–4 years old • Longitudinal study on operation

Sources: PAD (February, 2010); ISRs (February, 2011; May, 2011; December, 2011); ICR of related Basic Education Development Phase III APL-P085851 (June 2008); Holland and Evans (2010); Personal communication with Peter Anthony Holland (TTL) (November, 2012).
Note: ECD = early childhood development; IBRD = International Bank for Reconstruction and Development; ISR = Implementation Status and Results; PDO = project development objective.

SENEGAL: NUTRITION ENHANCEMENT PROGRAM (PHASES I AND II)		P070541; P097181
PROJECT DEVELOPMENT OBJECTIVE:	Phase I: *To improve the growth of children under three in poor rural and urban areas and build the institutional and organizational capacity to carry out and evaluate nutrition interventions.*	
	Phase II: *To expand access to and enhance nutritional conditions of vulnerable populations, in particular those affecting growth of children under five in poor urban and rural areas.*	
COMPONENTS:	1. **Community-based Nutrition and Growth Promotion Program** (Phase I and II)	
	1.1. Growth monitoring and promotion	
	1.2. Nutrition and health group education	
	1.3. Integrated Management of Childhood Illnesses	
	1.4. Basic health services	
	1.5. Fighting the roots of malnutrition	
	2. **Capacity Building and Monitoring and Evaluation** (Phase I and II)	
	2.1. Institutional and organization capacity building	
	2.2. Monitoring and Evaluation and research	
	3. **Multisectoral Support for Nutrition** (Phase II)	
PROJECT DEVELOPMENT OBJECTIVE INDICATORS:	1. Program coverage of children under the age of five in rural areas	
	2. Proportion of children exclusively breastfed until 6 months	
	3. Proportion of pregnant women and children under five sleeping under ITN	
SECTOR BOARD	Health, Nutrition, and Population	
STATUS	Active	
DURATION	11 years (Phase I: FY02–FY07) (Phase II: FY07–FY13)	
BORROWER	Government of Senegal	
TOTAL PROJECT COST	US$62.6 million (US$20.2 million in Phase I; US$42.4 million in Phase II)	
FUNDING	IDA credit: US$29.7 million; Government of Senegal: US$ 17.8 million; World Food Program: US$6.7 million; African Development Bank: US$4.5 million; UNICEF: US$3.3 million; Foreign multilateral institutions, including Canadian Government and European Union: US$600,000	
LENDING INSTRUMENT	Adaptable Program Loans	
TARGET POPULATION	1.7 million children below 5 years old/ pregnant and lactating women (Phase II)	
PARTNER AGENCIES	Cellule de Lutte Contre la Malnutrition; World Food Program, Ministry of Economy and Finance, UNICEF	
WB PROJECT MANAGER	Menno Mulder-Sibanda, Claudia Rokx	
ICR RATINGS	Outcomes: *Highly Satisfactory*	
	Risk to Development Outcome: *Low or Negligible*	
	Bank Performance: *Satisfactory*	
	Borrower Performance: *Highly Satisfactory*	
	(January 2007)	

table continues next page

(continued)

SENEGAL: NUTRITION ENHANCEMENT PROGRAM (PHASES I AND II)	**P070541; P097181**
RESULTS	• Reduced prevalence of severe underweight (21 reduction) • Reduced prevalence of underweight children below (44 reduction) • Increased proportion of children exclusively breastfed for 6 months (17–49) • Increased prenatal care use (at least three visits) (65–78) • Increased proportion of caregivers who recognize at least two danger signs in sick children (61–81) • Increased consumption of iodized salt (46–59) • Increased proportion of children sleeping under ITN (28–59) • Increased Vitamin A supplementation coverage of children aged 6–59 months (42–85)

Sources: PAD-P070541 (February, 2002); ICR- P070541 (January, 2007); PAD- P097181 (October, 2006); ISR- P097181 (September, 2012); Personal Communication with Menno Mulder-Sibanda (TTL) (December, 2012).
Note: IDA = International Development Association; UNICEF = United Nations Children's Fund; ITN = insecticide-treated bed net.

Bibliography

Banerji, A., W. Cunningham, A. Fiszbein, E. King, H. Patrinos, D. Robalino, and J. Tan. 2010. *Stepping up Skills for More Jobs and Higher Productivity*. Washington, DC: World Bank.

Cole, M., and S. R. Cole. 2000. *The Development of Children*. 4th ed. New York: Worth.

Denboba, A., R. K. Sayre, Q. Wodon, L. Elder, L. Rawlings, and J. Lombardi. 2014. *Stepping Up Early Childhood Development: Investing in Young Children with High Returns*. Washington, DC: World Bank.

Engle, P. L., L. C. H. Fernald, H. Alderman, J. Behrman, C. O'Gara, A. Yousafzai, M. Cabral de Mello, M. Hidrobo, N. Ulkuer, and the Global Child Development Steer Group. 2011. "Strategies for Reducing Inequalities and Improving Developmental Outcomes for Young Children in Low-income and Middle-income Countries." *The Lancet* 378 (9799): 1339–53.

Garcia, M., A. Pence, and J. Evans. 2008. *Africa's Future, Africa's Challenge: Early Childhood Care and Development in Sub-Saharan Africa*. Washington, DC: World Bank.

Glewwe, P., H. G. Jacoby, and E. M. King. 2001. "Early Childhood Nutrition and Academic Achievement: A Longitudinal Study." *Journal of Public Economics* 81 (3): 345–68.

Grantham-McGregor, S., Y. Bun Cheung, S. Cueto, P. Glewwe, L. Richer, B. Trupp, and the International Child Development Steering Group. 2007. "Developmental Potential in the First 5 Years for Children in Developing Countries." *The Lancet* 369 (9555): 60–70.

Grantham-McGregor, S., S. Walker, S. Chang, and C. Powell. 1997. "Effects of Early Childhood Supplementation with and without Stimulation on Later Development in Stunted Jamaican Children." *American Journal of Clinical Nutrition* 66 (2): 247–53.

Hasan, A., M. Hyson, and M. C. Chang, eds. 2012. *Early Childhood Education and Development in Indonesia: Strong Foundations, Later Success*. Washington, DC: World Bank.

Heckman, J. J. 2008a. "Schools, Skills, and Synapses." *Economic Inquiry* 46 (3): 289–324.

———. 2008b. *The Case for Investing in Disadvantaged Young Children, in Big Ideas for Children: Investing in Our Nation's Future*. Washington, DC: First Focus.

Heckman, J. J., and D. V. Masterov. 2007. "The Productivity Argument for Investing in Young Children." *Applied Economic Perspectives and Policy* 29 (3): 446–93

Holland, P., and D. Evans. 2010. *Early Childhood Development Operations in LCR: Jamaica, Mexico, and Brazil in Focus*. Washington, DC: World Bank.

Lefebvre-Hoang, I., and W. Cunningham. 2011. "Children and Youth Investments in the World Bank Portfolio, 2000–2010." *Child and Youth Development Notes* 4 (3).

Moss, P., G. Dahlberg, and A. Pence. 2000. "Getting Beyond the Problem with Quality." *European Early Childhood Education Research Journal* 8 (2): 103–15.

Naudeau, S. 2009. "Supplementing Nutrition in the Early Years: The Role of Early Childhood Stimulation to Maximize Nutritional Inputs." *Child and Youth Development Notes* 3 (1), Washington, DC: World Bank.

Naudeau, S., A. Valerio, M. J. Neuman, and L. K. Elder. 2011. *Investing in Young Children: An Early Childhood Development Guide for Policy Dialogue and Project Preparation.* Washington, DC: World Bank.

Neuman, M. J., and A. Epstein Devercelli. 2013. "What Matters Most for Early Childhood Development." SABER Working Paper Series No. 5, World Bank, Washington, DC.

Shonkoff, J., L. Richter, J. van der Gaag, and Z. Bhutta. 2012. "An Integrated Scientific Framework for Child Survival and Early Childhood Development." *Pediatrics* 129 (2): 460–72.

Vegas, E., and L. Santibáñez. 2010. *The Promise of early Childhood Development in Latin America and the Caribbean.* Washington, DC: World Bank.

Wang, Y., A. Denboba, M. McLin, M. Neuman, R. Sayre, and Q. Wodon. 2014. *Early Childhood Development for Policymakers and Practitioners: eLearning Course.* Washington, DC: World Bank.

World Bank. 2007. *Healthy Development: World Bank Strategy for Health, Nutrition, and Population Results.* Washington, DC: World Bank.

———. 2011a. *Education Sector Strategy 2020.* Washington, DC: World Bank.

———. 2011b. *Jamaica and Mexico Exchange Strategies for Early Childhood Development and Parent Support.* South-South Knowledge Exchange Hub. Washington, DC: World Bank.

———. 2012. *Resilience, Equity, and Opportunity: World Bank Social Protection and Labor Strategy.* Washington, DC: World Bank.

World Health Organization and UNICEF. 2003. *Global Strategy for Infant and Young Child Feeding.* Geneva: World Health Organization.

Young, M. E. 2001. *A Global Directory of Early Child Development Projects.* Washington, DC: World Bank.

Young, M. E., ed. 2002. *From Early Child Development to Human Development.* Washington, DC: World Bank.

Environmental Benefits Statement

The World Bank is committed to reducing its environmental footprint. In support of this commitment, the Publishing and Knowledge Division leverages electronic publishing options and print-on-demand technology, which is located in regional hubs worldwide. Together, these initiatives enable print runs to be lowered and shipping distances decreased, resulting in reduced paper consumption, chemical use, greenhouse gas emissions, and waste.

The Publishing and Knowledge Division follows the recommended standards for paper use set by the Green Press Initiative. Whenever possible, books are printed on 50 percent to 100 percent postconsumer recycled paper, and at least 50 percent of the fiber in our book paper is either unbleached or bleached using Totally Chlorine Free (TCF), Processed Chlorine Free (PCF), or Enhanced Elemental Chlorine Free (EECF) processes.

More information about the Bank's environmental philosophy can be found at http://crinfo.worldbank.org/wbcrinfo/node/4.